THE PIP ANTHOLOGY OF WORLD POETRY
OF THE 20TH CENTURY
VOLUME 5

GREEN INTEGER
6022 Wilshire Boulevard, Suite 200A
Los Angeles, California 90036

(323) 857-1115 fax: (323) 857-0143
E-Mail: info@greeninteger.com
visit our web-site: www.greeninteger.com

Douglas Messerli, Publisher

THE PIP

ANTHOLOGY OF WORLD POETRY
OF THE 20TH CENTURY

VOLUME 5

INTERSECTIONS: INNOVATIVE POETRY
IN SOUTHERN CALIFORNIA

Edited with an Introduction by
Douglas Messerli

EL-E-PHANT 5

GREEN INTEGER
KØBENHAVN & LOS ANGELES
2005

GREEN INTEGER BOOKS
Edited by Per Bregne
København / Los Angeles

Distributed in the United States by Consortium Book
Sales and Distribution, 1045 Westgate Drive, Suite 90
Saint Paul, Minnesota 55114-1065
Distributed in England and throughout Europe by
Turnaround Publisher Services
Unit 3, Olympia Trading Estate
Coburg Road, Wood Green, London N22 6TZ
44 (0)20 88293009

(323) 857-1115 / http://www.greeninteger.com

First Green Integer Edition 2005
Back cover copy ©2005 by Green Integer

The editor would like to thank the MFA Writing Program of Otis College
of Art & Design for their support, intellectual and financial, for the
publication of this volume.

Design: Per Bregne
Typography: Kim Silva
Photographs: [from top row to bottom, left to right]
Robert Crosson (Jeffrey Scales), Wanda Coleman (Douglas Messerli),
Diane Ward (Douglas Messerli), Will Alexander (Douglas Messerli),
drawing of Paul Vangelisti (Giuliano Della Casa), Martha Ronk (Marcel Shaine),
Jerome Rothenberg (©2001 by Christopher Felver),
David Antin (©2001 by Christopher Felver), Joe Ross (Douglas Messerli)

LIBRARY OF CONGRESS CATALOGING IN PUBLICATION DATA
Douglas Messerli ed. [1947]
The PIP anthology of World Poetry of the 20th Century, Volume 5
Intersections: Innovative Poetry in Southern California
ISBN: 1-931243-73-5
p. cm – Green Integer/EL-E-PHANT no. 5
I. Title II. Series

Green Integer books are published for Douglas Messerli
Printed in the United States on acid-free paper.

TABLE OF CONTENTS

INTERSECTIONS—INNOVATIVE POETRY IN SOUTHERN CALIFORNIA

For some years now I have considered editing and publishing the volume you have in your hands. There were several reasons why I felt we needed such a publication. First of all, the high quality and breadth of innovative poetry in Southern California impressed me as early as my first visit here in 1984, and the writing has continued to amaze and delight me in the twenty years since I moved to Los Angeles. At the same time, few of the poets included in this volume—that is writers I believe to be writing innovative work—have been included in the many anthologies of Los Angeles Poetry published over the decades.*

There are many reasons, of course, why editors might wish not to include the poets I have chosen in this current anthology, the most obvious being aesthetic differences. Particularly, in the earlier anthologies, some of the poets included here (Thérèse Bachand, Guy Bennett, Franklin Bruno, Catherine Daly, Barbara Maloutas, Deborah Meadows, Douglas Messerli, Harryette Mullen, Christopher Reiner, Joe Ross, Mark Salerno, Standard Schaefer, Pasquale Verdicchio, and Diane Ward) were not yet living in the Los Angeles area or had not yet established themselves as published poets.

---

* The 1972 *Anthology of L.A. Poets,* edited by Charles Bukowski, Neeli Cherry and Paul Vangelisti, contained the work of 18 Los Angeles poets, only two of which (Paul Vangelisti and John Thomas) I would describe as innovative and have included in the current volume. Similarly, Vangelisti's *Specimen 73,* published the very next year by the Pasadena Museum of Modern Art, contained work by the same two poets of the 12 poets represented in that volume. William Mohr's *"Poetry Loves Poetry"* anthology of nearly a decade later (1985) did somewhat better in representing innovative work, including seven of the 28 poets I've selected: Wanda Coleman, Martha Ronk (who at that time used her married name, Martha Lifson), John Thomas, Robert Crosson, Leland Hickman, Dennis Phillips and Paul Vangelisti. *Harbinger: Poetry and Fiction by Los Angeles Writers,* edited by Terry Wolverton and Benjamin Weisman, contained no poetry by the writers in this volume (to be fair, *Harbinger* included only work by poets appearing in that years' LA Poetry Festival, but that too says a great deal about the inclusion of these innovative poets in the Los Angeles poetry scene.) Most notably, Suzanne Lumis's and Charles Webb's *Grand Passion* of 1995—which she once described to me as "definitive"—contains poetry by 76 Los Angeles poets, only two of which are included in my volume: Wanda Coleman and John Thomas. Paul Vangelisti's *L.A. Exile,* published by Marsilio USA in 1999, focusing only on poets who wrote about "exile," included four of the poets of this volume, Martha Ronk, Paul Vangelisti, John Thomas, and Diane Ward. More recently, David Ulin's *Another City: Writing from Los Angeles* (City Lights, 2001) contains only Wanda Coleman of the selection in my volume. *Writing Los Angeles: A Literary Anthology* of 2002, also edited by David Ulin and published by the prestigious Library of America, again contains only Wanda Coleman from my selection. In 2003 Dana Gioia and Scott Tinberg published the Los Angeles anthology, *The Misread City,* which included of my selection, only Wanda Coleman and Mark Salerno.

The more local focus of the previous anthologies I have mentioned on Los Angeles also excludes poets I have included from San Diego and elsewhere in southern California. But even granting these exceptions, there is something curious about the exclusions I have indicated. If one also were to mention innovative writers who lived in Los Angeles, but who are not included in my anthology because they have moved away—writers such as Clayton Eshleman, Jack Hirschman (who appeared only in the first two Vangelisti anthologies), Fanny Howe, A. L. Nielsen, Jed Rasula (who appeared only in Bill Mohr's 1985 selection) and Julian Semilian—the absence of innovative writing in these previous anthologies becomes even more apparent. Add to this the concomitant exclusion of innovative writers in numerous local reading venues and the absence of media attention, and it becomes quite apparent that Los Angeles and southern California poets and readers have mislead—or, perhaps, "misread"—themselves with regard to what poetry is in this region.

Along with the fiction of several area writers, poetry has been generally presented as personal narrative, wacky stories, and revelations of catastrophe, as a kind of solipsistic writing about the "end of the world"—you know, the total chaos and destruction for which movies present Los Angeles to be deservingly destined.* As Paul Vangelisti has written in "The Mislaid City"—a review of the two most recent collections—"What we have [in these anthologies] is popular culture's representations, or more often simplifications of whatever literary life has come to the attention of the ubiquitous 'arts and entertainment' editors of the local press." Certainly, it is not the Los Angeles poetry scene my friends and I experience.

For several years, accordingly, I felt there ought to be another viewpoint, an antidote, if you will, to the many anthologies that had come before. I sought a collection of poetry that would reveal the exciting and stimulating writing and thinking that I have encountered in southern California over the years. Several times I began the slow editing process, imagining the poets I'd include and the context in which I'd present their work. But each time I backed away from the project, or. periodically postponed it.

There were several reasons I did so. First, I have never been interested in regional gatherings. The accident of location, although it certainly can be an influence upon one's writing and perceptions, seemed—given my national and international interests—myopic. Nearly all the poets I would have wanted to include had larger contexts within national and international audiences, and might find their work delimited if presented in a regional context. Few of the poets—in style, subject, or form—more-

---

* Among the numerous motion picture examples one might cite—*The War of the Worlds, Blade Runner, The Day of the Locusts, Miracle Mile, Earthquake,* and *Volcano*—at least two of these films specifically show the destruction of both my home and the Green Integer offices.

over, had much in common; the poetry itself—although original—was disparate. None of the commonalities of, say, the New York School, here existed. If anything, these poets all agreed that they did not represent, separately or together, a particular *kind* of writing. Influenced by figures and subjects as varied as the Negritude poets, "language" writing, Jack Spicer, Gertrude Stein, John Cage (another Los Angeles-born writer), the Russian Futurists, Shakespeare, art, music, and performance, there seemed to be only that "accident" of being in the same place that brought them together.

Yet, despite the disparateness of the writing, they were "together," and quite often—at readings, conferences, parties, lunches, dinners, and just plain fraternizing. Although perhaps no poet was friend to all of the others, all were interlinked by friendships. And many—both in San Diego and Los Angeles—had had close friendships with others for decades. Indeed, in the late 1990s, several of these poets and other writer friends regularly attended my Sun & Moon monthly salons (which were held from 1985 to 1999), a reading series organized by Guy Bennett, Franklin Bruno, Standard Schaefer and Christopher Reiner in Santa Monica, weekly dinners at the house of Dennis Phillips and Courtney Gregg in Pasadena, and annual poetry festivals organized by Paul Vangelisti for his magazine *Ribot*—the most memorable of which was a two-day event held on Santa Catalina Island. Rae Armantrout, Joe Ross, David Antin, Jerry Rothenberg, and other San Diego poets attended some of these occasions as well. And, although this series of regular encounters was impossible to sustain in the vast spaces of southern California, readings have continued in a series organized by Andrew Maxwell at Dawson's Book Shop in Los Angeles, readings supported by the MFA Writing Program of Otis College of Art & Design at The Mountain bar in Los Angeles's Chinatown, and conferences and other events at local colleges. In short, most of the poets included in this volume had long sustained a series of relationships that could only be defined as "a group."

Some of these friendships and relationships existed for more than twenty years. Jerome Rothenberg and David Antin have been close friends since their college days in the early 1950s. Leland Hickman was a force in Los Angeles poetry and friend to many of the poets in this volume from the 1960s to his death in 1991. Dennis Phillips, Paul Vangelisti, Todd Baron, Martin Nakell, and Martha Ronk all began friendships dating back to the late 1970s and 1980s. Standard Schaefer had been a student of Martha Ronk, Dennis Phillips, and mine at Occidental College. Barbara Maloutas and Mark Salerno were students of Paul Vangelisti, Dennis Phillips and mine in the MFA Writing Program at Otis College of Art & Design. At least one poetic couple had even been linked romantically—but we are fast approaching a private world of gossip. Let us just say, the interlinking friendships have been long and sustained.

My own connections with Los Angeles poets and what I shall call "adjacent" figures (poets, writers, professors and other individuals involved with this grouping who are not included in the current anthology) similarly went back several years preceding my arrival here in 1985. Diane Ward and I had a friendship dating back to Washington, D.C., where we participated in a literary reading group in the late 1970s. Joe Ross was a student of mine at Temple University in Philadelphia before moving near me in Washington, D.C. and then, later, with his wife Laura, to San Diego. I knew David Antin and Jerome Rothenberg for several years before I moved here, and my companion, Howard Fox, had shown the art of David's wife, Eleanor, in exhibitions in Washington, D.C. I published fiction by Sam Eisenstein, friend to these innovative poets and an attendee of many of these poetic functions, before I moved to Los Angeles. The noted critic Marjorie Perloff, another friend and influential figure to this group, was my professor at the University of Maryland, indeed, was the one who introduced me to poetry. I had been in correspondence with Leland Hickman (numerous poets in the East Coast regularly read his magazine *Temblor*) and Clayton Eshelman, whom I had published in my mimeograph journal, *Là-Bas*.

It is within this context that I came to reconsider what had brought these people together. Suddenly it became apparent that, even if their poetry seemed disparate, there were a great many common interests or foci that we all shared. I came to identify six such linkings—or what I have come to call "intersections" (in southern California location is often defined by major intersections of streets). No one figure shares in all of these "intersections," and some share only a few; but most of the poets included here are linked in a great many of their interests and activities.

Editing and Other Poetic Activities

What is perhaps most astonishing, given the absence of the work of these poets in Los Angeles anthologies and their invisibility in the "scene" as a whole, is the fact that it is precisely these poets who have been the most active in presenting the poetry of Los Angeles writers and others to the nation and to the world. Despite the misrepresentation of the recent Dana Gioia and Scott Tinberg anthology, wherein the editors claim "Los Angeles has never sustained a significant literary quarterly and few of the many (usually short-lived) journals contain significant numbers of essays or reviews," the truth is that Los Angeles and southern California has been blessed by a great number of intelligent journals and presses, the most important of which have been edited by the group represented in this volume. Perhaps a short history might permanently lay to rest such mistaken assumptions.

As Bill Mohr has pointed out in his essay in *Place As Purpose: Poetry from the*

Western States (Los Angeles: Autry Museum of Western Heritage/Sun & Moon Press, 2002), from the mid 1940s through the 1960s, with the exception of *Coastlines** and James Boyer May's *Trace,* the journals published in southern California—*Variegation, Recurrence,* and *California Quarterly*—were little known outside the region. Most of these journals focused on the local scene and, accordingly, had little national—certainly no international—readership. *Bachy*—a journal begun in the 1970s, published by John Harris, owner of the then popular bookstore, Papa Bachs—also focused in its earliest issues, edited by Bill Mohr, on the local. But in its last two issues, edited by Leland Hickman, and particularly in the last issue, *Bachy* 18, wherein Paul Vangelisti assisted in the international editing, the magazine came to be almost a model of what Los Angeles poetry publishing would eventually become. Along with local poets, the issue included a wide selection of nationally renowned writers and international figures.**

Previously, in 1971, Paul Vangelisti had begun one of the most important journals published in Los Angeles, *Invisible City*. The contents of that journal, ongoing for more than a decade, reads today like a who's who of national and international writing.*** The journal also contained extensive essays and correspondence, as well as specific poetic projects such as the Italian visual and concrete poetry collaborations of issues number 26-27 (1980).

Red Hill Press, co-edited by John McBride and Paul Vangelisti, brought the seem-

---

* *Coastlines* primarily represented the work of the "Deep Image" writers such as Robert Bly and a Los Angeles group of poets including Ann Stanford, Josephine Ain, Sanora Babb, Alvaro Cordona-Hine, James Boyer May, Bert Meyers, William Pillin, Thomas McGrath, and Mel Weisbrud.

** In order to establish publishing patterns, I have segregated local writers from what I often describe as renowned national writers; it should be made clear from the outset that many, if not most, of the local writers might also be perceived, in a different context, as writers of national importance. Examples of "local" writers in the last issue of *Bachy* were Robert Crosson, Kate Braverman, Dennis Cooper, Holly Prado, Jack Hirschman, Clayton Eshelman, Will Alexander, Martha Lifson (Ronk), Wanda Coleman, David Antin, Michael Davidson, Dennis Phillips, Charles Bukowski and Harry Northrop. Writers of national recognition included Robert Kelly, Tom Clark, Ed Dorn, and Garrett Hongo. Among the international figures represented were Rafael Alberti, Pablo Neruda, Vicente Aleixandre, Ernesto Cardenal, Aimée Cesaire, and Michel Deguy—to name only a few.

***A small list of the writers appearing in *Invisible City's* pages are Corrado Costa, Giulia Niccolai, Aldo Palazzeschi, Gilbert Sorrentino, Charles Bernstein, Heiner Müller, Bob Cobbing, Amiri Baraka, John Ashbery, Stuart Z. Perkoff, Tom Raworth, Adriano Spatola, Michael Palmer, Leslie Scalapino, Jack Spicer, Antonin Artaud, Henri Michaux, Hans Magnus Enzenberger, Bertolt Brecht, Walter Benjamin, Luis Cernuda, Nicholas Guillen, Federico García Lorca, Adonis, Yannis Ritsos, and Ewa Lipsa.

ing arch-enemies of San Francisco and Los Angeles together in its many volumes of international significance published from 1969 until 1989. Once again, as publisher, Paul Vangelisti included local and nationally renowned poets in the context of major international figures.*

After editing the famed *Caterpiller* in New York City and, later, in the Los Angeles suburb of Sherman Oaks, Clayton Eshelman began publishing *Sulfur* in 1981, supported originally by the California Institute of Technology in Pasadena, later by The Writers' Program of the University of California-Los Angeles and, finally, through National Endowment and California Arts Council support. Dennis Phillips was the book editor for the first nine issues, establishing one of the most prestigious sections of poetic commentary in the nation; that section would later be taken over by Jed Rasula and other correspondents such as Charles Bernstein, James Clifford, Marjorie Perloff, Jerome Rothenberg, Elliot Weinberger, and John Yau. One of the most highly respected poetic journals in the world, *Sulfur* published during its Los Angeles years (in 16 issues from 1981-1986) an enormous number of innovative poets and artists from the USA and abroad.** The journal also published major essays on many national and international poets and artists.

With the closing of *Bachy* in 1981, Paul Vangelisti (as Managing Editor) and Leland Hickman (as Literary Editor), along with Robert Crosson (as Assistant Editor) began a new journal of arts, *Boxcar*, in 1983. Once again, the two issues of this journal contained a broad range of contemporary poetry, including both figures involved with "Language" writing, significant American poets of national renown, and a wide range of local poets.*** Unfortunately, as the magazine attempted to gain the support of the local poetry center, Beyond Baroque, the editorial responsibilities

---

*   Local poets were represented in books such as *Geographies* by Robert Crosson and *Abandoned Latitudes,* with poetry by Crosson, John Thomas, and Paul Vangelisti. International figures and poetries were represented by books such as *Rimbaud under the Steel Helmet* by Helmut Maria Soik; *Various Devices* by Adriano Spatola; *Italian Poetry, 1960-1980: From Neo to Post Avant-garde;* and *Humps & Wings: Polish Poetry Since '68.*

** Among the hundreds of figures published in its pages were John Ashbery, Diane Wakoski, Paul Blackburn, Robert Kelly, Antonin Artaud, Harold Bloom, José Lezama Lima, Susan Howe, Cid Corman, Larry Eigner, Michel Deguy, Michel Leiris, Carl Rakosi, Lyn Hejinian, Michael Palmer, Clark Coolidge, Kurt Schwitters, Jackson Mac Low, Edmond Jabes, Laura (Riding) Jackson, Nathaniel Mackey, Valdimir Holan, and Arkadii Dragomoschenko.

*** Among the so-called "Language" poets were Lyn Hejinian, Michael Palmer, Bob Perelman, Bruce Andrews, Barrett Watten, and Ron Silliman. Other significant national figures included Robert Kelly, Rosmarie Waldrop, John Taggart, Helen Adam, David Bromige, and John Yau. Among the local figures were Robert Crosson, John Thomas, Paul Vangelisti, Martha Ronk, Dennis Phillips, Jed Rasula, Michael Davidson, Holly Prado, and Robert Peters.

shifted to a less focused editorial viewpoint, becoming the short-lived journal, *Forehead*.

In the long run the closing of *Boxcar-Forehead* was a fortuitous event, if one perceives both the last issue of *Bachy* and the two of *Boxcar* as trial-runs, so to speak, of Leland Hickman's important journal of contemporary poetry, *Temblor*—a journal with the most appropriate name for its earthquake-prone location and its national effects. Published from 1985 until 1989 for ten issues, *Temblor*, like its Los Angeles predecessors *Invisible City* and *Sulfur*, became one of the most talked-about journals in the United States. Following those two examples, moreover, Hickman combined the poetry of international figures with nationally recognized poets and work by most of the southern California poets then writing whom I have included in the present volume.* The journal also contained an extensive section of poetic commentaries, reviews, and correspondence, with highly memorable essays on several contemporary figures and issues. There is little question among innovative writers across the country that *Temblor* was one of the most significant poetry journals of the 1980s.

Shortly before his death of AIDS in 1991, Hickman's close friends Todd Baron, Dennis Phillips, Martha Ronk, and Paul Vangelisti attempted to develop a book publishing imprint under the *Temblor* name in his honor. The press never came to be, but after Hickman's death this group transformed the idea into Littoral Books, which, beginning in 1991, published several titles of local and nationally renowned poets.

From 1982-1986, Todd Baron and Tosh Berman edited a small poetry journal, *ISSUE,* and when that journal ceased publication in 1986, Baron began *Re*Map*, published from 1989-2001.

In the Washington, D.C. suburb of College Park, Howard Fox and I had begun *Sun & Moon Press: A Journal of Literature & Art,* a publication that would survive until 1982, when it was transformed into a non-profit literary press.** Beginning in 1978, the journal published two or three mimeographed books before turning its attention to hardbound and paperback works which as Sun & Moon Press relocated

---

* Issues included the work of Saúl Yurkevich, Pierre Guyotat, Bernard Noël, Minoru Yoshioka, Velemir Khlenikov, and Jacques Roubaud, along with nationally renowned figures such as Leslie Scalapino, Barbara Guest, Ron Silliman, Nathaniel Tarn, John Ashbery, Charles Bernstein, and Kenneth Irby—again to name only a few.

** Interestingly, while the journal published some international writers, its focus was primarily on American writing, and, while it published the work of several California artists (Channa Horwitz, Eleanor Antin, Allan Kaprow, Moira Roth, Joyce Cutler Shaw, and Norma Jean Deak), it published only three southern California writers, fiction writers Jeff Weinstein and Sam Eisenstein and poet Michael Davidson (and the work published by him was described as a fiction).

in Los Angeles, published over 350 books from 1984-2003, including, once more, a strong mix of significant American fiction writers and poets, local writers, and international figures.* Sun & Moon came to be recognized as one of the major independent publishers in the world.

The indefatigable Paul Vangelisti began a new journal, *Ribot*,** in 1993, published (with tongue-in-cheek) by CONS (The College of Neglected Science). In the eight issues of this wonderfully eclectic publication (it ended in 2002), he once again mixed international figures with national and area poets and the work of numerous artists, along with special issues on history and another on the nexus of poetry by young and older authors. As I mentioned previously, the CONS annual meetings became the *Ribot* conferences where over 50 poets met (one year on the nearby island of Santa Catalina, the second year at Otis College of Art, and the third year at Occidental College) to discuss varied issues of poetry and poetics.

In 1998, moreover, Vangelisti invited 21 poets, local and national, to contribute each month to the twelve issues that year of a journal titled *Lowghost.* More recently, from his position as head of the MFA Graduate Writing Program at Otis College of Art & Design, he has shepherded to press yet another new journal, *The New Review of Literature,* which includes Dennis Phillips, Martha Ronk, Standard Schaefer, Guy Bennett, and myself among its editors. The three issues of that journal to date include a hefty sampling of local, national, and international authors—poets and fiction writers—as well as a substantial review section with ten to fifteen titles reviewed in each issue.

From 1993 on Christopher Reiner edited a journal of poetic criticism and commentary, *Witz: A Journal of Contemporary Poetics,* which continued for a while on the internet.

---

* "Local" writers published by Sun & Moon Press include Dennis Phillips, David Antin, Paul Vangelisti, Rae Armantrout, Martin Nakell, Joe Ross, Jerome Rothenberg, Will Alexander, Martha Ronk, Guy Bennett, Standard Schaefer and Douglas Messerli. National and international figures include Paul Auster, Gertrude Stein, Djuna Barnes, Fanny Howe, Bruce Andrews, Barbara Guest, Steve Katz, Susan Howe, Lyn Hejinian, Mac Wellman, Russell Banks, Charles Bernstein, Nathaniel Mackey, Jaimy Gordon, André Breton, Raymond Queneau, Thorvald Steen, Henry Deluy, Inagaki Taruho, Arthur Schnitzler, Knut Hamsun, Anthony Powell, Tom Raworth, Valery Larbaud, and Arkadii Dragomoschenko.

** Issues have included work by Dennis Phillips, Rodrigo Toscano, Will Alexander, Marco Denevi, Nick Piombino, Leslie Scalapino, Charles Bernstein, Diane Ward, Sam Eisenstein, Giovanna Sandri, Todd Baron, Luigi Ballerini, Martha Ronk, Elio Pagliarani, Adonis, Mac Wellman, Norma Cole, Adriano Spatola, Nathaniel Tarn, Amiri Baraka and numerous others.

That same year, Mark Salerno began a handsomely produced "Magazine of the Arts," *Arshile*, which combined local, national, and international poets with the work of artists and essays on poetry and art.*

With Washington, D.C.-based poet Phyllis Rosenzweig, Diane Ward began *Primary Writing* in 1995, a journal of poetry that explores various formats mailed free to a list of recipients.

In 1997 Guy Bennett, the typographer for Sun & Moon Press, early Green Integer titles, and several of the other journals mentioned, began his own chapbook series, Seeing Eye Books, which publishes four annual titles, two of younger or major American poets and two of international figures.** Bennett is also co-publisher, with Paul Vangelisti, of a new press of critical and literary writing, Seismicity Editions, supported by Otis College of Art & Design.

Also in 1997, Standard Schaefer and Evan Calbi began the journal *Rhizome*,*** which published four issues, again following the Los Angeles model of local, national, and international poets. This journal also included art and a substantial number of book reviews in each issue.

In their early years, David Antin and Jerome Rothenberg were involved, through *Chelsea Review*, in literary publishing; in Los Angeles and San Diego, Martin Nakell, through his Jahbone Press, and Pasquale Verdicchio, in his Parentheses Writing series, have both published occasional books of local, national and international poetry figures. Joe Ross and others edited the magazine, *Zazil*, in San Diego.

More recently, Harryette Mullen rediscovered the hilarious novel, *Oreo*, by the Black writer Fran Ross, and saw to its republication. Will Alexander edited the poems of the beloved poet of Watts, K. Curtis Lyle.

Several "adjacent" figures have also edited important publications, among them Hans Jürgen Schacht, who published *Rowedder*, a journal of émigré writing and international poetry, and Andrew Maxwell, who with Macgregor Card, edited one of the most beautifully produced and voluminous journals, *The Germ*, which mixed

---

* *Arshile* has included work by Robert Creeley, Gilbert Sorrentino, Jack Hirschman, Mary Angeline, Michael Lally, Douglas Messerli, Carl Rakosi, Anselm Hollo, Peter Gizzi, Barbara Guest, and several international poets and artists.

** Writers to date have included Norma Cole, Dennis Phillips, Joe Ross, Clark Coolidge, Paul Vangelisti, Lyn Hejinian, Mohammed Dib, Giovanna Sandri, Hansjörg Mayer, Alfredo Giuliani, and Catriona Strang.

***Issues have included the poetry of Dennis Phillips, Bob Crosson, Leslie Scalapino, Guy Bennett, Martha Ronk, Douglas Messerli, Diane Ward, Paul Vangelisti, Barbara Guest, Tan Lin, Fabrio Morabito, Jaime Moreno Villarreal, Pierre Alferi, Timothy Liu and numerous others.

major national and international figures.

Finally, it is important to recall that from the mid 1960s until the 1970s, Black Sparrow Press, printing a wide range of national figures and a few poets of southern California such as David Antin, Charles Bukowski and Wanda Coleman, was located in Los Angeles, until its publisher, John Martin, moved first to Santa Barbara and, ultimately, to Sonoma County in northern California.

Several of the poets included in this volume, moreover, have edited major poetic anthologies, most notably Jerome Rothenberg. His editing alone might be said to constitute a whole library shelf of encyclopedic endeavors into various realms of national and international poetry.*

I have already alluded to several of Paul Vangelisti's many anthologies of local and international writing, including *Italian Poetry, 1960-1980* (edited with Adriano Spatola). With poet Martha Ronk, he also edited *Place as Purpose: Poetry from the Western States* and, with Luigi Ballerini (an "adjacent" figure living in New York but teaching at the University of California, Los Angeles), Beppe Cavatorta, and Elena Coda, Vangelisti edited *The Promised Land: Italian Poetry After 1975*, published by my own Sun & Moon Press.

Beyond the PIP series of international poetry, the fifth volume of which you hold in your hands, I have edited the well-received anthology *From the Other Side of the Century: A New American Poetry 1960 to 1990* and its companion volume (with Mac Wellman) *A New American Drama 1960 to 1995*. For two issues from 1993 to 1995 I edited *The Gertrude Stein Awards in Innovative American Poetry.* Various other poets included in this anthology have edited smaller collections.

I previously suggested the large number of readings and conferences attending the production of innovative poetry in southern California. Dennis Phillips was the director of the major Los Angeles poetry center, Beyond Baroque, from 1985 to 1988, and was responsible for its important reading series. David Antin, Rae Armantrout, Todd Baron, Guy Bennett, Michael Davidson, Deborah Meadows, Martin Nakell, Christopher Reiner, Martha Ronk, Joe Ross, Jerome Rothenberg, Standard Schaefer,

---

* Among his anthologies and gatherings are *Ritual: A Book of Primitive Rites and Events* (1966); *Technicians of the Sacred: A Range of Poetries from Africa, American, Asia, [Europe], & Oceania* (1967); *Shaking the Pumpkin: Traditional Poetry of the Indian North Americans* (1972); (with George Quasha) *America a Prophecy: A New Reading of American Poetry from Pre-Columbia Times to the Present* (1973); *Revolution of the Word: A Gathering of American Avant-Garde Poetry 1914-1945* (1975); (with Michel Benamou) *Ethnopoetics: A New International Symposium* (1976); (with Harris Lenowitz) *The Big Jewish Book: Poems & Other Visions of the Jews from Tribal Times to the Present* (1989); (with Diane Rothenberg) *Symposium of the Whole: A Range of Discourse Toward an Ethnopoetics* (1984); (with Pierre Joris) *Poems for the Millennium: The University of California Book of Modern & Postmodern Poetry* (1995/1998, two volumes); (with David Guss) *The Book, Spiritual Instrument* (1996); and (with Steven Clay) *A Book of the Book: Some Works & Projections About the Book & Writing* (2000).

and I, along with "adjacent" figures such as Aldon Nielsen, Andrew Maxwell, Hans Jürgen Schacht, and Luigi Ballerini have all organized reading series and conferences in and outside of the various institutions we represent.*

In short, this prodigious outpouring of poetic publications and activities may be the most defining aspect of the innovative poets from southern California.

International Perspectives

In the recounting of the publication histories above, I think it quickly becomes apparent that a majority of the southern California poets involved in publishing have also been committed to international writing. In a quick list of contributors to Vangelisti's *Invisible City* that I asked him to compile, he mentioned over 110 international poets writing in French, German, Italian, Spanish, Arabic, Dutch, Greek, Hungarian, and Polish. To date, my Green Integer press has published over half of its 115 titles from other languages.**

This interest in the international, moreover, goes much deeper than publishing. A substantial number of poets in this anthology, as well as "adjacent" figures, have been immersed in translation. Of course, one might observe in any large metropolitan area that a number poets are also involved in translation; but, particularly in this group of Los Angeles innovative writers, there is a commitment to translating that I feel goes beyond any such other literary gathering. Jerome Rothenberg is one of the most noted translators in the world, and has won awards for his translations of North American Indian writers, Kurt Schwitters (with Pierre Joris) and the Czech poet Vítêzslav Nezval (with Milos Sovak); he has also translated poetry and other works by Paul Celan, Günter Grass, Eugen Gomringer, Rolf Hochhuth, Federico García Lorca, Pablo Picasso, and Hans Magnus Enzensberger.

I have already recounted much of Paul Vangelisti's translating activities. Beyond the books I have already mentioned, Vangelisti has translated works by Amelia

---

* Such a flurry of poetic activity could not exist, of course, without the support of numerous institutions. Among these have been Art Center College of Design, The Autry Museum of Western Heritage, Beyond Baroque Foundation, CalArts (California Institute of the Arts), the California Institute of Technology, California State Polytechnic University, Pomona, Chapman University, the Contemporary Arts Educational Project, Inc, Dawson's Books, the French Consul to Los Angeles (Consul Général de France à Los Angeles), the Italian Cultural Institute (Instituto Italiano di Cultura), Occidental College, Otis College of Art & Design, Pasadena Museum of Modern Art, the University of California, Los Angeles Italian Department, the University of California, San Diego, University of Southern California, and Villa Aurora.

** These languages, many of them represented in bilingual editions, include Norwegian, Albanian, Romanian, Chinese, German, Polish, Italian, French, Spanish, Russian, Greek, Arabic, Japanese, Czech, Hebrew, Lithuanian, Finnish, Hungarian, Turkish, Korean, and Swedish.

Rosselli, Tiziano Rossi, Mohammed Dib, Rocco Scotellaro, Vittorio Sereni, Antonio Porta, and Giulia Niccolai.

Pasquale Verdicchio has translated books by several Italian poets including Antonio Porta, Emilio Villa, and others. Guy Bennett, who translates from French, Italian, and Russian, has published several works of translation, including books by Liliane Giraudon, Michel Leiris, Jacques Roubaud, Sergei Paradjanov, and Hans Bellmer. Mark Salerno has also translated from the Italian.

Several of the poets in this group who have not been directly involved with translation have nonetheless been highly influenced by the poetry of other countries, including Will Alexander, Deborah Meadows, David Antin, Dennis Phillips, Martin Nakell, and myself.

All this international interest, moreover, has not gone in just one direction. Other countries have invited several southern California poets to attend international conferences, and poets such as David Antin, Rae Armantrout, Guy Bennett, Wanda Coleman, Deborah Meadows, Martin Nakell, Dennis Phillips, Martha Ronk, Jerome Rothenberg, Paul Vangelisti, Pasquale Verdicchio, and I have traveled to countries as varied as Brazil, Cuba, the Czech Republic, France, Italy, Norway, Israel, Russia, Sweden, and elsewhere to read poetry at events such as the French Poetry Bienniele and the Milano Poesia Festival.

Given the linguistic activities of Paul Vangelisti, Pasquale Verdicchio, Mark Salerno, Guy Bennett, and Luigi Ballerini, the Italian connection has been a particularly fruitful relationship with southern California innovative poets, resulting, most notably, in a series of books edited by the Italian publisher Michele Lombardelli by Los Angeles poets and artists. To date, Lombardelli has published books in Italian and English by Robert Crosson, Dennis Phillips, Paul Vangelisti, Martha Ronk, Diane Ward, Guy Bennett, and myself.

One should further mention the international interests of a great many of the individuals whom I have described adjacent figures. These include Clayton Eshelman, Luigi Ballerini, Rick Gilbert, Michael Henry Heim, Marjorie Perloff, and Sanda Agalidi, all of whom have regularly attended events sponsored by the innovative poets, and who have been high influential to the group.

Guy Bennett, who married French scholar and writer Beatrice Mousli, organized a conference held in 2003 at the University of Southern California, Occidental College, and Otis College of Art & Design: "Charting the Here of There: French & American Poetry in Translation in Literary Magazines, 1950-2002," which included several Los Angeles innovative poets and contemporary French writers. Luigi Ballerini and Paul Vangelisti organized (with the University of California-Los Angeles, The Contemporary Arts Educational Project, and Beyond Baroque) a large Italian poetic conference in 1994, "The Disappearing Pheasant II," which included several contemporary Italian poets and national and local American writers (Part I had occurred in New York a few years earlier).

It is no coincidence, accordingly, that southern California innovative poets have been translated into numerous languages, including Dutch, Finnish, French, German, Italian, Romanian, Portuguese, Polish, Serbian, Spanish, and Czech.

Given this wonderful panoply of international poetic endeavors, one might almost be tempted to boast that southern California is the nation's "translation" center. Certainly, living in Los Angeles and San Diego, with its widely diverse populations and languages, one can well understand that the focus for innovative writers here is essentially international, and is, perhaps, the aspect that most distinguishes this group from any other American gathering.

Film, Drama, and Performance

Whenever one begins talking about Los Angeles and southern California one cannot ignore the numerous mythologies in which the area seems buried as deeply as in its reputed smog. Particularly when one discusses anything to do with Hollywood and the film industry, one quickly becomes mired in absurd visions of Los Angeles—visions often shared by Angelinos as well as outsiders. In part, the problem is the very complexity of the city and the art of living here. In a sense, all myths are true—there is always some grain of the truth in even the most ridiculous of constructions—and all the myths are simultaneously false.

The effects and power of the film industry in Los Angeles and environs is one of the most difficult of issues. If one looks at it only from the financial perspective, it appears, for example, that the film industry is the largest of southern California industries and we—just as Washington, D.C. is centered in politics—must be immersed in film. The figures alone are quite staggering: Walt Disney, for example, the largest publicly owned company in the area had 117,000 employees with sales of nearly $25,000 million dollars in 2001, and companies such as Dream Works SKG, Metro-Goldwyn-Meyer, and Univision Communications—the powerful Hispanic language television, internet, music, and media company—also posted staggering profits for that year—and these represent only four of the powerful entertainment organizations.*

---

* According to The Los Angeles County Economic Development Corporation, based on a comprehensive report of organizations employing 3,000 or more people in the Los Angeles five-county area in 2000, DreamWorks SKG employed 1,500 individuals with sales of $2,219 million dollars; Metro-Goldwyn-Meyer employed 1,000 individuals with sales of $1,388 million; and Univision Communications employed 2,400 employees, with $888 million dollars of income.

One must remember, however, that most of these companies are national and international in scope, and not all the employees are located in southern California. Indeed, when one looks at the picture from another viewpoint, from the perspective of what people actually *do* in the area or from how they are employed, entertainment quickly falls in the lists. Disney, the largest entertainment group, is ranked 12th of the largest 90 organizations, and only 4,799 people worked for the Walt Disney Studios and its Feature Animation divisions; ABC Inc, Anaheim Sports, Disney Consumer Products, and Disneyland Resort made up most of the remaining employees. By comparison, Los Angeles County employed 88,779 individuals. The University of Southern California had 53,065 employees. The Boeing Company, one of the major providers in the aerospace industry, had 38,000 employees. The health industry, led by Kaiser Permanente and Tenet Healthcare, far outflanked any entertainment group. The fact that 103,352 individuals were employed by the five largest university and college systems in the area presents a very different picture of Los Angeles from the many myths surrounding it.

My point in presenting all of this statistical information is simply that the film industry and entertainment does not dominate life in Los Angeles and southern California. While one may often spot movie actors and filming activities throughout the city, so too do the residents of New York, Vancouver, and Toronto. Life in Los Angeles—no matter how the film and media industries would like the world to believe it—does not center on filmmaking.

Although many innovative poets were involved in and influenced by film, accordingly, the perceptions they have had about it, particularly when it involves the Hollywood film factories, has not always been positive. Several figures "adjacent" to these innovative poets have worked in film. Julian Semilian was a noted film editor before he quit in disgust and what he described as "boredom" to teach film and film-making elsewhere. Thomas Roberdeau, a regular attendee of the Sun & Moon salons, scripted several films and teleplays, but for most his life—as for most of the screen-writers throughout the city—he has had to deal with failed promises and frustration. I recall the successful screenwriter, Nevin Schreiner, telling me—in response to my statement, "It must be rather frustrating to sell a screenplay and then never have it made into a movie"—"No, the frustration comes when a screenplay is made into a film." Studio head Irving Thalberg once described writers as "necessary evils," to which S. J. Perlman is reputed to have replied, "I think he means 'necessary weevils.'"

Todd Baron was a child actor, but did not pursue a career in films later in his life. He acknowledges the influence of film in his writings, but that influence comes from the film's form, and, in particular, its narrative intercutting. Robert Crosson delight-ed in expressing his hatred of his motion picture experiences in *White Christmas* and other movies, and throughout his work, including the longer poem "The Day Sam Goldwyn Stepped off the Train," there is a great deal of satire about the industry. Although many images of popular American films punctuate the poems of Rae Armantrout, they have been primarily negative ones, images such as that of Marilyn Monroe: "Those unwieldly bosoms held together by weak 'spaghetti straps.' …Something was inadequate. The squeaky little girl voice would never be able to articulate all that matter."

Paul Vangelisti began his career as a filmmaker in the mode of cinematographers such as Kenneth Anger, Bruce Connor, and others of the Canyon Cinema group. Though he loves to recall the gossip about film people from his days as editor and reporter for *The Hollywood Reporter,* his poetry has rarely contained images or even made mention of American films or filmmaking.

Christopher Reiner has made independent films, but his poetic narratives are inspired more by Baudelaire than by American filmmakers. Married to scriptwriter Chris Hauty, Diane Ward has referred to film in her book *Imaginary Movie,* but once again, it is the movie as form in which she is interested:

> a composed corner's distance
> differentiation and room
> the outsides
> duration of such a moment
> cinematic orthodoxy
> for the money and of the moment

Previously, in New York, Ward worked with independent filmmaker Henry Hills, and she has made clear that her cinematic preferences are for his kind of intimate filmmaking.

With his wife, artist and cinematographer Eleanor Antin, David Antin co-scripted the independent film *Music Lessons,* which he has described as an attempt to create a "crossover" movie; accordingly, "it had a fairly straight-forward narrative plot" but was "highly eccentric in theme and language."

Dennis Phillips also began his career working with movies; involved with the Los Angeles Independent Film Oasis, Phillips co-directed the experimental documentary *Possibilities of Activity* with Tony Forma, and for several years after worked as a sound recorder for films and documentaries. He has described his sound editing experiences as being influential, but only in an oblique way, to his poetry.

Guy Bennett and "adjacent" figure Marjorie Perloff both briefly worked on translating film dialogue. Bennett is a great admirer of international filmmaking—he introduced me the work of Sergei Paradjanov, whose *Seven Visions* Green Integer published—but his poetry is perhaps influenced more by photography and architecture than by film.

Martin Nakell and others (including "adjacent" figures Andrew Maxwell and Fanny Howe) are knowledgeable devotees of 20th century films, but once again, it is international film that has been the most influential on their work. As a graduate student at the University of Maryland, I briefly taught film, and taking advantage of my own library of tapes and videos of American and international films, I have watched at least one film daily for the past several years. Yet in only one book, *Along Without*, subtitled a *film for fiction in poetry* do I involve my writing with film. And here again the form, a kind of closet-film no one could ever visually realize, is more important than traditional film influences. Like several of the other poets whom I have mentioned, my love of film is focused on international directors such as Bergman, Fellini, Fassbinder, Bresson, Renoir, Kurosawa, Buñuel, Rivette, and Tarkovsky.

Perhaps only Thésèse Bachand, who worked as continuity editor on the movie *The Black Stallion,* has extensively used images of Hollywood movies in her poetry, *luce a cavallo (a portrait of selves),* in which she "writes through" movies of the 1960s. But here, too, the focus is primarily on international pictures. Her interest in American films *(Three Days of the Condor, Klute, Chinatown, Women in Love, Bedazzled,* for example) is based on the fact, she explains, that many of the studio films of the 1960s were directed by individuals who looked to international films and, in their independence, helped ironically, temporarily to save the studio system.

In short, while the film medium has been highly influential to a number of the innovative poets in southern California, their focus—despite living at what many see to be the center of American filmmaking—is once again on the international.

Some of the poets in this anthology have been involved with drama, and their poetry reveals that relationship. But, as with film, their connections with this genre have been largely tangential to the numerous large and smaller theaters throughout southern California.

From 1977 to 1983 Paul Vangelisti was executive producer of the nationally syndicated radio-drama series, "The Los Angeles Theater of the Ear." Beginning with Peter Handke's "Offending the Audience," plays were broadcast monthly in live coast-to-coast readings through National Public Radio.* Two Pirandello adaptations were

---

* Among the playwrights included were Frederich Dürrenmatt, Harold Pinter, Samuel Beckett, Mario Diament, Corrado Costa, Stanislaw Lem, Ntozake Shange, Amiri Baraka, David Hare, Ernst Meister, Flann O'Brien, and others.

new translations of *Six Actors in Search of a Director* and *Henry IV,* and in 1980 Vangelisti adapted James Joyce's *Ulysses* for radio performance, which won the Corporation for Public Broadcasting's Drama Award. Vangelisti was also involved in performances with the Los Angeles Actors Theater and other groups such as the East/West Players. He directed Robert Crosson's play "The Party: Reunion," William Wintersole's adaptation of Djuna Barnes's *Nightwood,* and a large-cast reading of my performative work, *The Walls Come True: An Opera for Spoken Voices,* in which Robert Crosson acted.

Dennis Phillips studied drama with Herbert Blau at CalArts in his college days, concentrating on the theater of Grotowski. Lee Hickman, trained as a professional actor, performed in plays in his New York City years, most notably in a one-man performance of Shakespeare's *Henry IV,* which he recreated later, at Phillips's request, at CalArts. Joe Ross's first poetic work, *Guards of the Heart,* was made up of four short plays, two of which were performed in Washington, D.C.

As a twelve and thirteen year old, growing up in the midwest, I memorized information—names of plays, directors, theaters, and the number of performances—from the Burns-Mantle books of *Best Plays* from 1900 to the early 1960s just as my peers memorized baseball cards, and I was an avid reader of plays by Pinter, Ionesco, Beckett, and Albee. It was only later in my life, after I had published several books of poetry, that I began to write plays; to date I have published one longer play, *The Confirmation,* and seven shorter plays in a volume titled *A Dog Tries to Kiss the Sky.* Only one has been performed in Los Angeles, but others have been staged in New York, San Francisco, and São Paulo, Brazil. In the late 1990s my publishing house and non-profit organization, The Contemporary Arts Educational Project, Inc., presented readings, in collaboration with the Los Angeles theater group Bottoms Dream, of numerous plays by contemporary dramatists.*

The series lasted for two years, during which time I felt that in these unstaged events, I was witnessing some of the best of contemporary drama. In 1998 I edited, with Mac Wellman, a large selection of 38 plays titled *From the Other Side of the Century II: A New American Drama 1960-1995,* which continues to be a standard text for drama courses across the nation.

Home to some of the most exciting performance art in the country—art that shares more links, perhaps, with visual mediums than with the sequentiality of drama—southern California has also been one of the centers of performance art in poetry.

---

* Readings of works by Mac Wellman, Erik Ehn, Jeffrey Jones, Naomi Iizuka, John O'Keefe, Djuna Barnes, and many others occurred over a period of the two years.

David Antin, whose wife, Eleanor, is also a major performance artist, has been very much the center of the connections of performance with poetry. His "talk poems," as he describes them, generally begin with an invitation to speak at a particular location and to a specific audience; often there is also a specific occasion involved. With these variants in mind, Antin contemplates various subjects, and then, at the occasion, speaks improvisationally, recording his comments on a tape recorder. Antin is a born storyteller, and the performances, accordingly, often consist of numerous shorter tales of family, friends, and events in his life. His work, produced when he later rewrites and edits his talks for the page,* has been described by some readers as short fiction or "comic monologues." To see the work as either, however, is to miss most of the texture and form of the work. As Marjorie Perloff has described "Definitions for Mendy" (included in this volume)—a precursor of his "talk poems"—Antin uses various devices such as "associative rhythms," fragmentation of phrasing, suspension of meaning, repetition of words and other tropes found in more "traditional" forms of poetry.** Although his work cannot be scanned and is not broken into lines or even the paragraph units of prose poetry, his improvised performances constitute poetic events.

Jerome Rothenberg often has included elements of "sound" poetry—devices taken from the native American Indians and sound poets such as Kurt Schwitters— in his poetic performances.

Linked perhaps more to drama than to pure performance, Wanda Coleman's readings also have been described as performance events. Similarly, in their lengthy structures and relationship with chants and spells, the poems of Will Alexander often bear a close relationship with performance poetry.

Into several of my own poetic readings, I have woven dramatic episodes and other performance elements; with David and Eleanor Antin, Jerome Rothenberg, Michael Davidson, and Pasquale Verdicchio I performed in La Jolla a long section my performance work previously mentioned, *The Walls Come True*.

Film, drama and performance are central, in short, to several of the poets included in this volume, but in most cases, their interest has been toward the non-traditional manifestations of these genres.

---

* Through the use of a lower case typography, punctuated with breaks to indicate natural breaks for breath or other verbal emphasis, Antin's written text maintains much of the feeling of a spoken text.

** For a fuller discussion of Antin's "talk poems," see Perloff's *The Poetics of Indeterminacy: Rimbaud to Cage* (Princeton, New Jersey: Princeton University Press, 1981), pp. 288-339.

Visual Art

It would be a safe to suggest, I would guess, that all of the poets included in this volume have been influenced, at one time or another, by visual art and, in particular, the rich tradition of the arts in southern California. But the intersections that tie these writers together go far deeper.

Will Alexander is a painter, Paul Vangelisti a noted collagist. I have had my collages shown at art galleries in the area. Jerome Rothenberg and David Antin, it is important to note, taught for many years in the art department at the University of California, San Diego; Paul Vangelisti, as I mentioned previously, heads the MFA program at Otis, and Guy Bennett and Barbara Maloutas also teach there; Dennis Phillips teaches at Art Center College of Design in Pasadena. Barbara Maloutas, Dennis Phillips, and Diane Ward all graduated from art schools. I have lived with the curator of contemporary art at the Los Angeles County Museum of Art for some 30 years, and over those years have regularly been involved with museums and galleries; Dennis Phillips is married to a visual artist.

Several of the journals I spoke of in discussing the first intersection—Mark Salerno's *Arshile,* Vangelisti's *Invisible City* and *Ribot,* and my own *Sun & Moon: A Journal of Literature and Art,* as well as the adjacently related journal, *Sulfur,* all contained hefty sections devoted to art in each of their issues. I have already spoken of the collaborations with Los Angeles poets and artists represented in Michele Lombardelli's Italian series of book publications.* These same poets have been involved in numerous other collaborations over the years supported by local institutions and galleries.

The Landscape and Language of Southern California

A few of the poets share an interest in the very landscape of southern California, that is the flora and fauna of the region. At least two critics, for example, have noted that Rae Armantrout incorporates a great deal of local landscape, creating in her poems a world of "oleander," "scrawny palms," "empty streets and loose, flapping leaves." "Columnar / palms and junipers [sway] / toward or away from one another;" "Pigeons bathe in technicolor fluid 'of a morning.'" Bird-of-paradise plants and cactuses pepper her poems.

---

* Among the Los Angeles artists with whom these poets collaborated were William Xerra, Courtney Gregg, Don Suggs, Tom Wudl, Michael C. McMillen, Ron Griffin, and John Baldessari.

Similarly, in the poems of Martha Ronk one finds images of "cactus pears," the "Mohave," "doves calling from the palm tree," catalogues of street names, "Line up like nouns, names like Avocado, Orangegrove, Lemontree...." "Between Eagle Rock and downtown drops away / before the freeway loops / and manzanita signs off reddish / in the pale light before rushhour...," writes Ronk about the "no man's land" of that landscape.

"East Bakersfield winters trees strip & go / dusty-blank, the sky / oilsmoke- / blank, vacant lot foxtails sick white ochre," writes Leland Hickman in *The Great Slave Lake Suite*; elsewhere in the same poem: "reborn fresh morning spring creekside bird- / sung proud paleblossomd owl-home wingd-ant-home snake-home, song-home, my kiss-the-ground sanctum blackwillow."

"What life and death: watching a mockingbird trying to distract two crows from the nest," observes Paul Vangelisti in his prose-poem *Nemo*. "First time this morning I see a hummingbird;" "Wind shakes bushes and trees and what has been. / Flock of blackbirds shivers to the west. / Another Pacific storm on the way, the radio says...."

So too, in the work of Dennis Phillips, the sea and southern California landscape play an important role:

> It was a sign of good planning
> to see how quickly the flora and fauna
> rebounded from domestic treatment.
>
> The rippling sound of fronds.*

In his newest work, Guy Bennett writes of the local architecture: "Built blue to house bright forms, scale the surrounding," "Floating the city this house captures, 180 cavelike, completely glazed."

In my own recent poetry, "there is a kind of sweetness in the chill, a jacarandaed scent that settles over ahead."

In short, in numerous works by these poets the varied landscape of southern California—with its high and low deserts, ocean, forest, vast dusty tracts of land, and interminable bright, yellow-white light—has crept into what is otherwise quite dissociative writing. But as both Brenda Hillman and Fanny Howe have noted in describing Rae Armantrout's work, although images of flame and flowers, of birds and swaying trees abound, "Eden has disappointed itself and fallen. ...This is like

---

* Dennis Phillips, from "Keahole," in *Study for the Ideal City* (Los Angeles: Seeing Eye Books), p. 37.

southern California whose garden says no."* "When a landscape doesn't confirm your idea of the nature of the universe," writes Howe, "it might as well be hell."**

Anyone who has even visited southern California must realize that this region has no distinct dialect, no obvious distinguishing aspects of speech. Indeed, made up as it is of a populace from all over the nation, from all the world, the English one hears in southern California is closest, perhaps, to the bland, uninflected speech of the western edge of the Midwest, of Nebraska and Kansas. So, to talk about a southern California "language" seems almost ridiculous. Consider, however, the five selections below:

> What the cool tomato cubes forming a rosette around this
> central olive have to do with love and happiness.

> An eclipse spills water
> knots, its eventual illusion
> a bubble.

> Each promise or statement equals a temptation
> and yet holding to a story can often create history.

> The dead start where the dream never did...

> Avoidance proper is a verb conjugated in another tongue
> in routine and repetitive fashion in an Italian hilltown
> in which buildings wind their bricks in circular motion
> around relic fingerbone anchored in silver filigree.

Each of these passages—from poems by Rae Armantrout, Guy Bennett, Dennis Phillips, Paul Vangelisti, and Martha Ronk—shares several linguistic elements with the others. At the heart of each, there is a kind of maxim-like statement that sounds a bit like an old wives' tale or an aphorism. There is, moreover, a delay in the logic of

---

* Brenda Hillman, "Crossing the Garden re: Rae Armantrout's Metaphysics," in *A Wild Salience: The Writing of Rae Armantrout,* edited by Tom Beckett (Cleveland, Ohio: The Burning Press, 1999), p.47.

** Fanny Howe, "The Garden of Even," in *A Wild Salience: The Writing of Rae Armantrout,* edited by Tom Beckett (Cleveland, Ohio: The Burning Press, 1999), p. 51.

each phrase, which along with an inversion of the usual order and/or extension of metaphor, almost obscures the sentence structure: in Armantrout's phrase, one almost loses the sense of "the cool tomato cubes" having to do with "love and happiness" through the insertion of the second metaphor "central olive" and the gerund phrase "forming a rosette around." So too, in the delayed modifying phrase in Bennett's statement about "water knots," with the final metaphor "bubble" saved for the very last of sentence; the structure of Phillips's sentence, "holds the story" from its beginning "promise"; and in Vangelisti's sentence, the end ("the dead") begins a sentence which, in most cases, would have begun with "the dream." As Ronk's selection indicates, there is an "avoidance," as if the noun were being trans-lated into another language or another possibility of meaning before the sentence is completed.

If this seems a little far-fetched, consider two further examples:

> Will even before
> touch perspires
> stills assumption.

> The people above ground inhabit the complex—the
> proliferation of the rabbits is very much threat and
> nuisance to.

The selections from my own work and that of Robert Crosson's both, once again, hold the story and reconsider its meaning, before delivering an aphoristic punch.

Of course, the similarities I am pointing out may simply be ones of influence; perhaps these poets have influenced each other; Gertrude Stein, moreover—who has had a impact on most of the poets—could be said to have very similar patterns in much of her writing. I would like to suggest, however, that these linguistic patterns are due to something else influenced by the experience of living in southern California; but before I can speak of that, we should perhaps consider the last of what I describe as "intersections," that of narrative.

Narrative

Diane Ward—perhaps the poet least concerned with narrative in this volume—recently recounted, "When I moved here and began reading the poetry of my friends, I was amazed at how narrative the work was. What is all this interest in narrative, I asked myself?"

Several of the poets in this volume also write fiction: Will Alexander, David Antin (who, as I mentioned, is often thought of as a fiction writer), Wanda Coleman, Robert Crosson, Barbara Maloutas, Martin Nakell, Dennis Phillips, Martha Ronk and I have all written works of short and longer fiction. Leland Hickman's poetry, moreover, has often been described as long, narrative monologues; Christopher Reiner's prose poems could also be thought of as short works of fiction; and both Paul Vangelisti and John Thomas have written longer narrative-based poems.

I want to make it clear, however, that when I am speaking of narrative, I am not speaking of "storytelling," but of the sequential aspects of the poetry. These poets are not doing what Ezra Pound warned of, simply telling stories broken into short lines, but are incorporating narrative, with its structures of repetition, episode, catalogues, brief remembrances, and, yes, sayings and aphorisms, into their works. I think one could say that, to a certain degree, these narrative devices appear in the writings of the majority of the poets in volume, particularly in poems by Alexander, Antin, Armantrout, Bachand, Baron, Coleman, Daly, Davidson, Hickman, Nakell, Reiner, Ronk, Ross, Rothenberg, Salerno, Thomas, Vangelisti, Verdicchio, and my own work. Even in the poetry of Dennis Phillips, where most seeming narrative connections have been erased, the work retains a strong sense of narrative possibility and urgency.

As I noted earlier, the work is not representative of the more story-based poetry that has appeared in many of the anthologies of Los Angeles and southern California poetry. But, when I first moved here, at time in which my friends connected with "Language" writing were eschewing these very tactics, I also wondered—despite the fact that my own poetry had always contained narrative devices—why this should be.

After a few years of living here, I became convinced that it had something to do with time and space, with the time one had to spend in the automobile and the space one transversed through the region simply to arrive at one's place of employment, let alone to attend a reading or share an evening with friends. There was something about moving through that space in time that broke experience up into small segments, as one passed through different communities and parts of the city.* In the end, one experiences a city like Los Angeles a bit like the photography of Robert Flick, who photographs the major boulevards block by block and pieces them

---

* For those unacquainted with Los Angeles, one must understand that the city is not filled with vast empty sprawls like those of some western communities. Indeed, over the years of the city's existence, buildings have been constructed upon almost every inch of available space, high into the canyons, right up to the ocean's edge. But neither is the city one vast metropolitan experience. Within the confines of Los Angeles city are other communities, neighborhoods like Brentwood, "Little Tokyo," "Little Ethiopia," "The Miracle

together into a vast, collage-like frame running from left to right in rows. The effect is to create a narrative that has no true connections other than the fact that it represents the visual integrals as one travels through these avenues. If one does this daily, I surmised, it effects the way one perceives life. Life—at least life as lived in a car—becomes a series of narrative experiences. And that, in turn, had affected these poets. (I live, I should note, one block away from my office.)

More recently, however, I have become convinced that it is not just traveling through the area that creates this experience, but actually living in it. Not only is the face of the city constantly in change,* but as social observer Norman Klein and others have observed, southern California is an area that standardly forgets itself. As each new wave of immigration alters the makeup of the city, so too are the shared experiences and institutions of the earlier times forgotten. What might once have seemed of immense importance to a Black citizen of Olympic Boulevard in midtown has little meaning, perhaps, to today's Korean-American. The white working-class gathering spots of citizens of Alhambra can have little importance for today's Chinese-Americans living there. In short, the city is not only an architectural perplexity, but it also a social conundrum.

Accordingly, in attempting to understand this city, one must travel out from one's own neighborhood in all directions, day by day piecing the constantly shifting pieces of a puzzle together. For newcomers this is daunting task. The story has often been told: after spending months of traveling through various areas of Los Angeles to get to know the city, the new resident chances a drive up into the canyon to see what might be there. Suddenly, having climbed to Mulholland Drive, he witnesses the valley on the other side as it comes into view—there before him is another city, nearly as vast as the one from which he has just come!

Mile," where I live, as well as actual cities within the larger city such as West Hollywood, Beverly Hills, Culver City, Venice, Pasadena, Malibu, and Santa Monica. Moreover, while on the major streets, (Pico, Olympic, Wilshire, Beverly, Santa Monica, Melrose, Hollywood, Robertson, La Cienega, Fairfax, La Brea, Highland, Western, etc.) high rise buildings, restaurants, shops, theaters, museums, clothing stories, nail salons, theaters, synagogues, churches and other various commercial locations appear in a kind of hodge-podge array; one street away from these major thoroughfares are quiet residential neighborhoods. Finally, each of these are punctuated by the differences in communities, their constituencies, financial abilities, and regulations which make for an extremely varied experience as one moves from east to west, south to north. In a sense, there is no way one can assimilate all the variances. There is simply too much to assimilate.

* One of the newest trends in construction, particularly with homes in Beverly Hills, is to buy a nice large home of the past, tear it down and build a mini-mansion.

Robert Flick, *Melrose Avenue* [detail]

The only way anyone wanting to comprehend the experience of living and surviving in southern California can come to terms with the place is to create a narrative of sorts, to piece together the area, bit by bit, sharing small common experiences with friends. Where do you shop for food? What are your favorite restaurants? Outsiders often misunderstand these questions as a lack of the Angelinos' and San Diegoans' ability to engage in serious discourse. But these are important and significant questions in a constantly shifting world. I recall one time when poet friend Bruce Andrews was visiting Los Angeles he asked where he might go for contemporary music and dance. A mutual friend replied, "Well that's difficult, you see, because the venues change every night. Through word of mouth and e-mail the participants share the newest locations for each night's events."

Narrative becomes a survival strategy, a way of making sense of the overload of visual and temporal possibility. At the same time, it allows one to make sense of the past, to piece together what was once here, and where it has gone.

Those same narrative patterns are apparent in the linguistic examples I suggested were shared by several of the southern California poets. There is a sort of delayed history in the very structure of those sentences, an historical wisdom that is understood only by going *through* the entire thinking process of each new idea; to repeat:

> Each promise or statement equals a temptation
> and yet holding to a story can often create history.

Conclusions

After reading an early version of what you have just finished, a friend observed that were this not an historically-based introduction, but rather an essay, one might reverse the entire structure to reveal that the poetic concerns with narration these writers have assimilated through living in southern California might also be described as the very reasons why they have been so active in publishing (explaining that experience) and drawn to translation and international perspectives (attempting to comprehend it). I responded that, indeed, that probably was the case. The region, in fact, might be represented by the Ouroboros: as any innovative poet concerned with narrative knows, the good writer must swallow his own tale. If I make my way for an hour and a half through traffic and the urban landscape to attend a dinner party in Pasadena, I know that later in the evening I must reverse the voyage if I want to return home. In his poem "Questions from the Gates," Martin Nakell expresses this experience aptly in poetic form:

Were you actually inside the gates?

Yes. Some

Did you put your eyes
back in your pockets
like the rest of them?

No. I put them back
where eyes come from.

Why?

Because I had to come back here
to see you, to talk to you
about things.

Would you go back?

You mean inside those gates, where we both have been?

Yes. Back, inside.

What gates?

*

One might have chosen any number of other "intersections" between the poets in this volume: music, politics, food…. It should be apparent, nonetheless, that the group which I once felt—along with several of the poets in this volume—had no center, has had, at least, a strong gravitational pull. This, in turn, has made for a sense of shared experiences, not necessarily coherent or unified experiences, but ones that have brought these several poets together in numerous ways and allowed them to create—in a climate far different from what Stravinsky described as Los Angeles's "splendid isolation"—exciting, individualized poetic visions.

In a time where the culture at large, the media, and even serious readers seek the simple, things that are easier to explain and comprehend, the kinds of interrelationships I have just recounted, all centered in a complexity of issues, brings one to understand—while nonetheless regretting the reasons—why these innovative writers have been largely ignored by their own community and are unknown to others. Los Angeles and southern California has, after all, had a long tradition of ignoring its literary heritage, as well as other aspects of its culture. One only has to think of all the thousands of writers who have lived here*—long forgotten by most of the regions' denizens—to understand why these poets will perhaps continue to struggle in obscurity. Perhaps this volume will at least remind some readers that there was once such a group of devoted and committed poets in their midst.

Given the historical information and personal data throughout this volume it should be apparent that I have worked in close collaboration with all the poets contained herein, and I wish to thank them for their friendship and openness. Paul Vangelisti, in particular, served as a source of information that made this volume possible. Bill Mohr, who, having just completed his PhD dissertation on the poetry of southern California, was also an important source.

This book was conceived, in part, through a course I taught at Otis College of Art & Design in 2003. The students in that class—James Ayala, Melea Meyer, Nicole Moore, and Magdalena Saucedo—helped in the selection of the poets and interviewed several of the poets.

Kim Silva made the complex job of putting together the mélange of various materials a seemingly easy and coherent process. Diana Daves, once again, served as my eyes and ears. Charles Bernstein and Martin Nakell offered important editorial suggestions. Thanks to Robert Flick for allowing us to reproduce a detail from his photography. I also would like to thank the numerous individuals mentioned throughout my text as "adjacent" figures. These scholars, translators, professors, curators, artists, and friends have not only helped to sustain the work of these innovative poets of southern California, but have encouraged the poetic "group" to expand their thinking and practice into various other creative endeavors. Finally, I must again thank, along with the poets, the many institutions (listed on page 17) that have made publications, readings, and other events possible.

—DOUGLAS MESSERLI

---

* For a partial listing of the numerous writers—remembered and forgotten—who spent long periods of time in Los Angeles, I refer the reader to Paul Vangelisti's *L.A. Exile: A Guide to Los Angeles Writing* 1932-1998 (New York: Marsilio Publishers, 1999) and to Stephanie Barron's exhibition catalogue, *Exiles and Emigrés: The Flight of European Artists from Hitler* (Los Angeles: Los Angeles County Museum of Art, 1997).

Will Alexander [USA]
1948

Born and raised in South Central Los Angeles, Will
Alexander grew up around the violence that has
plagued this area for decades. The only child of
working class parents, he attended Washington
High School, avidly participating in school sports.
In 1972 he graduated from the University of Cal-
ifornia Los Angeles with a Bachelor of Arts degree
in English and Creative Writing.

In the mid-1970s the noted Black poet K. Curtis
Lyle, a founding member of the Watts Writers
Workshop, met with Alexander and others at his
home and at an incense business run by musicians
Ray and Ernest Straughter. This period was also
marked by a twelve hour dialogue in San Francisco with the surrealist poet Philip Lamantia
which had an enormous effect on him. Through those gatherings Alexander began confirm-
ing the power of works of his readings of Bob Kaufman, Octavio Paz, and Francophone
Negritude writers such as Aimé Cesaire and Jean-Joseph Rabéarivelo—all poets who would
strongly influence his subsequent poetry and, later, the visual art he had begun creating. Their
themes of cosmic isolation from society and interior discovery strongly affected him, and
helped him to what he describes as an "alchemical metamorphosis," which drew him away
from his intense involvement in sports to his participation in the arts.

In 1987 he published his first book, *Vertical Rainbow Climber,* which already contained the
heady mix of metaphor and sophisticated language that characterizes so much of his work. A
short chapbook, *Arcane Lavender Morals,* followed in 1994, with new books-including *The
Stratospheric Canticles, Asia & Haiti, Above the Human Nerve Domain,* and *Towards the
Primeval Lightning Field* following throughout the 1990s. This writing represents a complex
distallation of images from many fields, including botany, astronomy, psychology, phisiology,
mysticism, and history. He has also written novels and dramas.

Alexander has performed throughout the country, and has taught courses at the
University of California at San Diego, Naropa in Boulder, Colorado, and Hofstra University.
He was the recipient of a Whiting Fellowship for Poetry in 2001 and a California Arts Council
Fellowship for Poetry in 2002.

BOOKS OF POETRY

Vertical Rainbow Climber (Aptos, California: Jazz Press, 1987); *Archane Lavender Morals* (Buffalo: Leave Books, 1994); *The Stratospheric Canticles* (Berkeley: Pantograph Press, 1995); *Asia & Haiti* (Los Angeles: Sun & Moon Press, 1995); *Above the Human Nerve Domain* (New York: Pavement Saw Press, 1998); *Towards the Primeval Lightening Field* (Oakland: O Books, 1998)

from "Haiti"

"...these undistingushed dead
become known as that anonymous
heritage, les Morts."
            Maya Deren
            Divine Horesemen: The Living Gods of Haiti

"We
bubonic
with blackened altering transmissives
with burning nerve length & schisms
twisted in piercing soils
in dark pre-maturity & rage

we the dead
we the pressure & the cyclone of Haiti
savage with usurption
with clastrophobia by scarob
by blood loss & groaning
we who've taken spikes from our entrails
from suns we've had exploded in our nostrils
we who were spawned in harassment
in catastrophic silicate meanderings
in acidic neural complexity
corrupted & slashed
in lightless x-ray vacuums

we who swelter in cold & heatless malachite
in blatent triangle missives
in throughtless inversion & drought
above burning shells of crab
above a flood of random burial law
like cobras
or gazelles
or eaglets ruined in stunted cemetary icons

it is we who speak
with a sun of splinters spewing from our heart
from our thorax burning with intestinal moray explosion

we
the Africa of Songhai & Mali
we
of original reptile wisdom
we
the first gatherers of wool
through sun
through apertures spinning
in a ruptured lighning gorge

we
the dead
who blister
who channel poltergeists from lightless peeling rums
as spies
as wild omega charges
beyond ruthless murdering dossiers
beyond the Tontons & their terror
we float
above abcess torrents
above the bloody belladonnas
& the microbes & their seas
so we emit
lesser bodies of dying
lesser holocaust driftings
therefore we burn
in the bloodless heat of whispers
in stony cloves & disjunctives
in raw botanical monsoons

whenever the crops boil & disease themselves as acid
there is malaria by forgery
starvation under gemstone
as if treachery had been launched
throughout a shadow of bodies
throughout the reign of ominous modernity
where we shift between sulphur & limbo
between plaintive spillage & body
because

there is a discourse of bodies
of chapaarral by misnomer
of splendiferous mirage
& blistering anti-edict

we the dead
transcripting ruin & vapour
with demonish lisping trot
with slavos
by diorama & plague
by the very principle of pain
split apart & cyclonic

as for the souls of our two former killers
Papa Doc
with his rotted & greenish blood
with his consort
the Madame
ailing in her rubies & bones
we accuse them
with every quarter of their accursed mandibles
with every despicable vibration as owls
their gestures
their veins as leopards turned around in a mirror
grown from themselves lashing out as monsters

we see them now
throughut a wrenching prolapse through the kingdoms of hell
caged by the demons
within the macerated bones of mutual self-bleeding
…

(from *Asia & Haiti*, 1995)

The Impalpable Brush Fire Singer

No
he is not an urn singer
nor does he carry on rapport
with negative forces within extinction

he is the brush fire singer
who projects from his heart
the sound of insidious subduction
of blank anomaly as posture
of opaque density as ash

he
distanced from prone ventriloqual stammer
from flesh
& habit
& drought

the performer
part poltergeist & Orisha
part broken in-cellular dove
part glance from floating Mongol bastions

where the spires are butane
where their photographic fractals are implanted with hypnosis

because he allegedly embodies
a green necrotic umber
more like a vertical flash or a farad
posing like a tempest in a human chromium palace

therefore his sound
a dazed simoom in a guantlet
a blizzard of birds burned at the touch of old maelstroms

because he gives off the odour of storms
this universal Orisha
like a sun that falls from a compost of dimness

out of de-productive hydrogen sums
out of lightless fissures which boil outside the planet

yes
he sings at a certain pitch
which has evolved beyond the potter's field
beyond a tragic hummingbird's cirrhosis
surmounting primeval flaw
surmounting fire which forms in irreplaceable disjunction

under certain formations of the zodiac he is listless
he intones without impact
his synodic revelations no longer of the law
of measured palpable destinations
because he sings in such a silence
that even the Rishis can't ignore

as though
the hollow power which re-arises from nothingness
perpetually convinces
like a vacuum which splits within the spinning arc of an
intangible solar candle

such power can never be confusedly re-traced
because
it adumbrates & blazes
like a glossary of suns
so that each viral drill
each forge
casts a feeling
which in-saturates a pressure
bringing to distance a hidden & elided polarity

like a subjective skill
corroded & advanced
he sings
beyond the grip of a paralytic nexus
where blood shifts

beyond the magnet of volume
where the nerves no longer resonate
inside an octagonal maze
stung at its source by piranhas

(from *Above the Human Nerve Domain*, 1999)

Inside the Ghost Volcano

With the body of a morbid hanging doll
my aura burns
by shifts
by ambles
by mirages

by the sun in its primordial morass
summoned from a spectral locust feast

through electric bartering grammes
living
as if a spectrum had been transmogrified
across the sum of exploded solar windows
amidst motions of viral infamy
of sudden discharge pontoons
of magical lyncean sails above ships of pure vitrescence

enthralled
by empty Minoan game dogs
debating oxygen as form
debating menace as ideal
as one listens to fire
in dense eruptional gullet
in hanging hydrogen mirrors
so that each image is shifted
back & forth
between gales & the apparition of gales

so that
unicorns from Çatal Hüyük
cease to condense as forms of the earth
but take on the body of enigma as transparence
as blackened meteor in abstraction
the sun no longer quantified
by strange caledrical posses
but becomes
balletic differential
which ceases to quarrel
with the magic of fragment as schism

as mist
as a power cast before oasis

because the game dogs
the unicorn mirrors
spun as a wakeless ocular thirst
as a conjured distance
evolved from the force of a clarified activity

like darkened water as shock
as scale which looms as humidity
then the eyes always focused
as pleas for hushed exhibits

(from *Above the Human Nerve Domain*, 1999)

Impulse & Nothingness

These dense geranium surges of thought
protracted through steaming anthrax waters
concerned with the coronal aspects of contingency
these sabbatical athanors in which nothingness looms
without image

without the doctrinal plummage of a fixed event
without the mesmeric square of Talmudic rigidity
when one is transfixed by intention
by the the Messianic force fused with the illusive intensity
of impulse
shot into the grainy broach of nothingness

there exists the sense of bleached equators
the suicidal aching of secondary sunfish

one then gives off the odour of a pentacostal heresy
& one no longer lives in an aura of the weakened
with the weakened
one stands like a bolt
upright
facing the electrical debris of an ochlocracy in pain
staggered by the knife of its own surgeon's riddles
by a rabid scalpel cutting at its ribs
by a deboned pleurisy rumbling in its vision

as I reach into this nothingness
I am abandoned by associates
psychically spat upon by contemporaries
a reflex
against one condemned by the interests
of the secular nerve field

this I
a target
with an intense circulation of acid in the veins

so everything that I snare
always half plunged into eclipse
all my description
subject to electro-ballistical analysis
an analysis of my own achievement
which ironically has no power to engulf me

so I remain suspended
between light & the imageless arcana of extinction
& the emotions
those electrical cadavers
weave themselves like sickened medicine in my thorax

as to my name
it has become an exploded ravens' dyscrasia
an excresence
walking around with my eyes
like a series of neurological sunspots

& in speaking
I remain corroded with intensive tedium rejoinders
with my bones squirming at an angle of pathological
nightmare edicts
a cauldron of metacarpel tsunamis
as a result
I feed on the carking magnificence of lonliness
on the nomadology of cacti & sores

I count my companions as enemies
those obedient nomenciator's covering up those abbreviated
prolusory murders of the spirit

& so as a scar
as one given up to the guerilla domain of
cosmic prolepsis
I am always a figure
a metal hormone found in a basket
floating on broken sea bird's blood

on both sides of my eyes a parenthetical numbness
a painful but voided exogen climaterics
in which I wander through intensive flytrap grasses
weaving myself to death while humming in-doctrinal ballets
a shapeless fumatory witness

suffering like a cipher
or a metamorphic anagram
spying on shapes in the darkness

(from *Impulse & Nothing,* unpublished)

PERMISSIONS

From "Haiti"
Reprinted from *Asia and Haiti* (Los Angeles: Sun & Moon Press, 1995). Copyright ©1995 by
Will Alexander. Reprinted by permission of Sun & Moon Press.

"The Impalpable Brush Fire Singer" and "Inside the Ghost Volcano"
Reprinted from *Above the Human Nerve Domain* (New York: Pavement Saw Press, 1998).
Copyright ©1998 by Will Alexander. Reprinted by permission of the author.

"Impulse and Nothingness"
Reprinted from the manuscript, "Impulse and Nothingness," unpublished. Copyright ©2004
by Will Alexander. Reprinted by permission of the author.

David Antin [USA]
1932

Born in New York City in 1932, David Antin grew up
in Brooklyn in a family of European émigrés. His
father died when he was two, forcing his working
mother to leave him for years at a time with various
uncles and aunts who, as he remembers it, argued
and told endless stories in various European lan-
guages. These early family experiences are the sub-
ject of many of Antin's later "talk poems," and were,
in part, what helped him later to be such a gifted
storyteller himself.

DOUGLAS MESSERLI

As a young man he attended Brooklyn Technical
High School with intentions of becoming a scientist
or an inventor. It was there he read works such as
Gertrude Stein's *Three Lives* and Joyce's novels, all of which highly involved him, and began to
interest him a literary career. At age 16 he left home, ultimately attending the City College of
New York. There he met fellow student Jerome Rothenberg, a poet who still remains a close
friend of his in southern California. At City College he edited the the school's literary maga-
zine and wrote mostly fiction.

His ability with languages helped him to get jobs after college as a scientific translator.
When Rothenberg returned from the army, they helped found—along with Ursule Molinaro,
Venable Herndon, and Robert Kelly—the *Chelsea Review*. During that same time, Antin had
begun to write poetry, and responsive to Rothenberg's ideas of "deep image," began working
on an exploratory, expressive poetry that had an "image core." When the term was taken up by
others such as Robert Bly, Antin and Rothenberg felt that their ideas were "eviscerated" of any
intellectual significance, and they stopped using it. During this time of the early 1960s, his
poetry began to be published in various journals, including *El Corno Emplumado, Folio, Kayak,*
and *Trobar*—one even in *The New Yorker*.

Meanwhile, in December 1961, he married Eleanor, who later became an internationally
recognized artist. Antin became disengaged with the kind of writing he was doing and turned
from imagistic based works—works which critic Marjorie Perloff has argued owe something
to Surrealism and Breton—to a "process poetry," work influenced by the art world of the
1960s—much of which Antin was writing about in art journals—which was more "confronta-
tional" than the lyrically-based work he had been doing. In 1968 he published *Code of Flag
Behavior* and, in 1971, *Meditations* built around an alphabetical lising of words that high school
children had trouble spelling.

The same year, Antin was asked by Dore Ashton to take part in a series of talks she was
organizing at Cooper Union, and, along with other talks he was asked to do (at Pomona
College in Southern California and a reading at the San Francisco Poetry Center) Antin began
working with the improvisatory compositions that have defined much of his poetic activity

from 1972 onward. These pieces generally begin with a suggested topic, which, after research into various related subjects, are created before the audience as Antin interweaves various ideas and stories together through poetic devices such as repetition, rhythm, metaphor, and other poetic conceits. The pieces are taped and later typed up and revised by the poet into works that look more like prose pieces, albeit without margins and standard capitalization. Among his important books of "talk poems" are *Talking* (1972), *Talking at the Boundaries* (1976), *Tuning* (1984) and *What It Means to Be Avant Garde* (1993).

In 1968—on the day that Robert Kennedy was shot and killed in Los Angeles—the Antins moved to southern California to become professors of art at the University of California at San Diego. Thirty years later they continue to live in La Jolla.

BOOKS OF POETRY:

Autobiography (New York: Something Else Press, 1967); *Definitions* (New York: Caterpillar, 1967); *Code of Flag Behavior* (Los Angeles: Black Sparrow Press, 1968); *Meditations* (Los Angeles: Black Sparrow Press, 1971); *Talking* (New York: The Kulcher Foundation, 1972), reprinted by (Normal, Illinois: Dalkey Archive Press, 2001); *after the war* (Los Angeles: Sparrow, 1973); *talking at the boundaries* (New York: New Directions, 1976); *whos listening out there* (College Park, Maryland: Sun & Moon Press, 1979); *tuning* (New York: New Directions, 1984); *Selected Poems: 1963-1973* (Los Angeles: Sun & Moon Press, 1991); *What It Means to be Avant Garde* (New York: New Directions, 1993)

The Death of the Platypus

The sickness of crystal weighed on the mind of the platypus
With the heaviness of water and the half-lives of stars
Under his fur he remembered the rain of the meteors
And he cried for the creatures of the earth's first night
The platypus cried in his subtle voice of giraffes
For the white kingdoms of chalk and the abandoned coral cities
He cried for the passing ferns and the chaste maidenhairs
He cried for the blindness of molluscs and the deafness of fish
He cried for unlit stone lilies at the sea bottom
And for the Arctic poppy and rose
The platypus cried for brave beginnings
For the launchings of sea snails and for hummingbirds lost at sea
He cried for victims
For the sea mice preyed on by cod and for krill
He cried for lemmings under the snow
The platypus cried for the killers
For insatiable shrews and starving weasels
He cried for the spendthrift seed
For the glut of salmon spawn and the lost flags of dandelion
He cried for the sorrows of parents
For the dead infants of sea otters and bereaved sea horses
For drowned seal pups and smashed eggs in the rookeries
He cried for the frangible wings of insects
The elytra of beetles and the nervures of flies
He cried for the spongy antlers of deer and the hollow narwhal horn
He cried for heavy bodied birds
For condors that must wait for the wind and for moas stuck in the mud
He cried for the foolish ground pigeon and the lonely solitaire
The platypus in his great grief cried without discretion or measure
His tears sank deep into the ground where they corroded aluminum
And his great heart caved in like the quenched walls of the sun.

(1959)

Touch

Only a touch!
—Whitman

soiled like gauzes
like bolts of cloth in warehouses
scraped and worn
fingered like money and moons
lips and knees skinned
by bricks that are rich in abrasions
in overripe fruit
let go of my hand in this fetid jungle of pain
with its false legs
and rubber bandages
where the tall steel birds are picking the bones of the night
the smell of wet timbers rotting
standing water
chalkdust of blackboards that never come clean
and the writing of one word
is blurred by the word underneath
that never wiped off
of desks with names cut into their skins
of birds made of smoke
of glass
of glass
of glass
hands wearing endlessly at the hardness
of glass that isn't the hardness of ice
or of steel the desert of glass
the waterless glass
the tree seen through bars of glass
the snarl of its roots
trapped between gutters of blood
the tree of pain blasted by glass

(1960)

constructions and discoveries

morning and the jib of a crane
today the air is full of breaking things
things
rising and falling
full of angles and ladders
bright powder
pollen and chalkdust
in the sunlight

men in bright helmets
raise structures
proffer hopes
on scaffoldings
the city is full of its projects

a claw hangs over a wall
the heart drops in its cage
like an elevator
and I was looking for you
among shadows of courtyards
trying to find your face
behind a wall made of doors
on a ruined staircase
with mirrors
among fallen stones

I was looking for you at night
in bus terminals and on stations
in hospitals full of sick children
in parks with dead grass and drowned statues
in dark windows
where is the tree that stood outside your window last night
that now is a wall
a wall that is yellow and pink and blue
the helmets are silver

by the river the children
are selling pictures to men in white suits
pictures of your face

at night along the wall
there are flares
drills and detonations

the sun breathes on the beach in a dish
like the heart of a mollusc

under the cover of night
the light congeals to a fruit
that no one dares eat
the night is covered with snow and cut hands

(1961)

regarding a door

regarding a door
its open and shut
but it is less open and shut than a wall
a wall is something to lean on
and its unwise to lean on a door
regarding a door
you can take it in hand
turning the knob of a door you can open it and step through
then its no longer a door
now in the case of a wall
it's a wall wherever you are
which is evident and consoling
with a wall you always know where you are
while a door is only a door from outside
there is also something substantial about walls
maybe it's the materials from which theyre made

the bricks and the plaster
but more likely its the absence of hinges
the hinges in doors are like hidden conditions
upon which everything turns
theyre like the small print in contracts
a door depends on its hinges
but it also depends on a wall
theres nothing unusual about a wall without doors
a door without a wall is ridiculous
also a door is usually visible in all of its limits
but you cannot see the other side of a wall
and a door is always suggesting another side
so doors seem ambiguous and appear to be forever flapping in the wind
a revolving door seems to be always changing its mind
but regarded from whatever angle
it is always offering you the same proposition
there are many unanswered questions about doors
why is it that there arent circular or elliptical doors
what is it thats frightening about sliding doors
and what about the colors of doors
green doors in brick walls
white doors in black walls
or black doors in any walls
this will lead you to suspect that i am talking about
symbols
rather than about doors and walls
whats all this talk about doors and walls anyway
why not talk about something real
like strainers

(from Code of Flag Behavior, 1968*)*

code of flag behavior

the flag should never be displayed with the union down   except
    as a sign of distress
the flag should never touch anything underneath it
such as the ground   the floor   or water
it should never be carried laid out flat or horizontally
but always aloft and free
it should not be festooned   drawn back   or up in folds
but allowed to fall free
the flag should never be used to cover a ceiling
it should never have placed on it   or attached to any part of it
any mark insignia letter word figure design picture drawing
of any nature whatsoever
the flag should never be used as a receptacle for
receiving holding carrying or delivering
it should not be used for advertising purposes   and
when the flag is in such condition that it is no longer fit for use
as an emblem of display
it should be destroyed
in a dignified way
preferably by burning

(from *Code of Flag Behavior,* 1968)

transformation 2

the men
cannot go anywhere

they are doomed
to making pictures

by turning
swinging
and twisting the ropes

this quickly wearied
the watcher

a nail
driven into a wall

a house
hung over a hill

seemingly

      suspended

          in space

on wooden trusses
reinforced concrete

use music to help paint a picture

a word to cover a table

such as

redwood

jackhammers

of

the lure of a presence
unseen
but familiar

(from *Code of Flag Behavior,* 1968)

Definitions for Mendy

loss is an unintentional decline in or disappearance of
        a value arising from a contingency
a value is an efficacy a power a brightness
it is also a duration

to lose something keys hair someone
we suffer at the thought
he has become absent imaginary false
a false key will not turn a true lock
false hair will not turn grey
mendy will not come back
but longing is not imaginary
we must go down into ourselves
down to the floor   that is not imaginary
where hunger lives and thirst
hunger imagine bread   thirst imagine water
the glass of water slips to the floor
thirst is a desert
value a glass of water
loss is the glass of water slipping to the floor
loss is the unintentional decline in or disappearance
        of a glass of water arising from a contingency
the glass   pieces of glass
the floor is a contingency
the floor is a floor
is a contingency
made of wood
the fire is a contingency
the bread is burned
burning is not a contingency

the presence of the dead is imaginary
the absence is real

henceforth it will be his manner of appearing
so he appears in an orange jacket and workpants and a blue
                                        denim shirt
his hair is black his eyes are black
and a blue crab is biting his long fingers
he is trying to hold the bread
he is trying to bring the water to his mouth
his mouth is a desert
the glass of water will not come
the glass of water keeps slipping through his fingers
the floor is made of wood it is burning
it is covered with pieces of glass
arising from a contingency
his face is the darkened face of a clock
it is marked with radium
the glass is falling from his face
the face of a clock in which there is a salamander
whose eyes are bright with radium
radium is a value that is always declining
radium is a value that is always disappearing
lead is also a value
but it is less bright than radium

loss is an unintentional decline in or disappearance of
        a value arising from a contingency
a value is an efficacy a power a brightness
it is also a duration

is there enough silence here for a glass of water

is it dark enough for bread
take a glass of water
hold it against a wall
it is not pure water
it is almost pure wall

glass   what is glass

glass is a solution
of sand and chalk and ashes
fused by fire
it is a desert
that transmits light

the thirst is not appeased

water is a barrier

a glass of water is between us
you are there and i am here
is it a corollary of the fact that two things cannot
      be at the same place at the same time
that two things can be at two different places at the
      same time

you are there and i am here and i see you
but you are changed
two things at the same place at two different times
where you were the floor is empty
there is no shadow on the wall
i can only see the wall in my mind
i am not where i was then
but i still see your shadow the glass on the floor

in all matter there is an innate force
a power of resisting

take a glass   fill it with water

the thirst is not appeased

take a glass of water
drop it on the floor
it smashes
it is wood and glass and water

the thirst is not appeased

a glass of water falling
is a falling body of water
and obeys the laws of falling bodies
according to which
all bodies fall
at a rate that increases   uniformly
regardless of their form or weight
at the same altitude and latitude
the weight of a body   is the force
with which the earth   pulls the body down
mendy weighed one hundred and thirty-seven pounds
which is to say
that the earth   pulled mendy down
with a force equal to that

exerted upon a mass of one hundred and thirty-seven pounds
at forty-five degrees latitude
at the level of the sea
the earth pulls all bodies down

the thirst is not appeased

i am trying to hand you a glass of water
i am trying to give you a piece of bread
i cannot give you anything
there is a glass of water between us
i can only see you by the light the glass lets through

there is a piece of bread between us
if we could only see it

no one doubts the efficacy of bread
bread is a power
if we could only release it
it is a body
containing light

there is a piece of bread between us
break it
bread is a barrier

bread is a body
water is a body
the earth is a body
the sun is a body
a clock is also a body
light is a body   of a sort
what sort   it is heavy and falls
three hundred and sixty tons of light fall
from the sun on the earth every day
physics imagines a black body
a black body gives back no light

             •

duration
it is a stone
it is a fact
it does not move
it has no place into which it could move
it has no place to move out of
it is a stone
it is a face
it is a stone on which water has dropped
it is a face
it is hard
it is smooth
the water does not wear it away
it wears the water away
it is a fact
it does not mean anything
it cannot tell time

•

it is a fact

not having seen you for a long time and you
didn't live far away you came to see me in the
winter it was cold in my apartment which was
heated with gas and you wore a scarf to keep
warm when i asked you what you were doing you
said you were sick and i said we were all sick
and it didnt matter but you said you were really
sick you were dying and i asked you how did it
feel because i didnt know what to say and
you said it felt queer

•

yellow
branches of willow
small flames of forsythia

soft air
        black water
     caressing the branches
         sun
       overhead

     •

it is a fact

to hear the Grosse Fuge and Webern and the
great fugue was a great distance away like a
square masted ship tossed in a storm in an
old painting and the Webern was close and
dazzling   light glancing off glass and water
we came back in the rain i never saw you again
it is important to learn what the eye can see and the
    ear can hear

to record the truth

taking pictures of trees
the fountain of elm branches a spray of silver now
last of the maidenhairs timbre of a voice
drops of water sounds decaying on the air

choose/to fix a body in space
choose/unaccelerated axes
choose/a frame to fix a face

the eye cannot discriminate true intensities of light
only their ratios
similarly the ear
cannot distinguish among sounds that are very high or low
in the dark all cats are black
what color are they in a blinding light

(The initial definition of *loss* is
quoted from p. zz of Mehr and
Cammack's *Principles of Insurance*.
The initial definitions of value are
from *Webster's New International
Dictionary,* the 1927 revision)

"Chalk, fine sulfide of arsenic and pow-
dered verdigris can be thrown among the
enemy and all of those who inhale the
powder as they breathe will be asphyxiated.
But make sure you have the wind behind
you."

Leonardo—Notebooks

Tabun, Sarin and Soman are three lethal
nerve gases developed by the Germans at
the end of the second World War. They are
colorless, odorless and can kill by landing
on the skin. The last two are currently
being stockpiled by the Russians and
Americans among a variety of more
sophisticated biological weapons.

(from *Code of Flag Behavior,* 1968)

first meditation

1. making a claim is by implication a form of acknowledgment. by
making this kind of claim one is making this kind of acknowledgement.

2. if one takes a photography one lets it develop. when the face of a
woman appears you are content because it is what you expected to develop.

3. if the picture turns out badly you call that an unexpected development.
when there is no picture at all its more unexpected but not what you would
call a development.

4. a man with a mission to fulfil goes away to fulfill it.

5. the mission succeeds or it doesnt and he bases his judgment on what doesnt happen. he says it is on the basis of what hasnt happened that he makes his judgement.

6. the man with a guitar in his hands outside of a window is lovable. but if there is no light in the window is he more or less loveable?

7. when a photograph appears in a window it is marvelous. it is marvellous to return from a mission with a photograph.

8. one must admit to oneself it is marvelous to return with a woman. how much more marvellous to return without one's self!

9. there is something suspect in the pleasure of overcoming resistance. that there may be less interest in pleasure than the resistence.

10. to leave what you are not able to do is a way of being skilful that leaves no room in it for any other way of being skillful.

(from *Meditations*, 1971)

meditation 4

if a sick man enters a house the members of the household are all more or less susceptible to his disease   and it will spread by contact from the infected to the uninfected   and each infected will run the course of his sickness and recover or die of his sickness   and his chances to recover or die of his sickness will vary from day to day in the course of his sickness   and his chances of conveying his sickness to the uninfected will vary from day to day   as the sickness spreads there will be fewer and fewer members who may become infected   one day the sickness will come to an end

(from *Meditations*, 1971)

meditation: west

the soldiers were in the habit of saying that a dying soldier was "going west"   are
you going west on your vacation?   we turned west at Allentown and drove west-
ward for several hours   their motto was "westward ho!"   the suffering in the near
east was desperate

(from *Meditations,* 1971)

Rae Armantrout [USA]
1947

Born in a naval hospital in Vallejo, California in 1947, Rae Armantrout began life and was reared in communities of military men and their families on naval bases throughout California, but predominantly in San Diego. As an only child with a deep sensitivity to her own inner life, she lived a very insular childhood, described quite beautifully in her short autobiography of 1998, *True.* Like many young, developing writers and artists, Armantrout felt distanced from the lives of her parents, but her parent's fascination with myths of the West, balanced with a Methodist fundamentalist perspective gave Armantrout a strong sense of irony, revealed in nearly all her poems.

NANCY WOLFING

Living with her parents in the working class community named Allied Gardens, Armantrout enrolled at San Diego State University in 1965, with the intention of majoring in anthropology. During her first year there, she met Chuck Korkegian and continued to date him throughout her university years in San Diego. During her sophomore year she discovered the works of poets such as William Carlos Williams and Denise Levertov, which led her to refocus her educational studies on English and American literature. Ultimately, this led her to transfer to the University of California, Berkeley.

While attending the university in Berkeley, Armantrout studied with Levertov and made friends with Ron Silliman and others who would eventually be connected with the San Francisco group of "Language" poets of the late 1980s. She graduated from Berkeley in 1970, returning to San Diego and Chuck, whom she married in 1971. With a few poems accepted by Clayton Eshelman for his magazine *Caterpillar,* Amantrout began to perceive herself as a poet.

She went on to take a Master's degree from San Francisco State University, publishing her first book of poems, *Extremities,* in 1978. Since that time she has been actively involved in various literary communities through southern California. Among her books are *The Invention of Hunger* (1979), *Precedence* (1985), *Necromance* (1991), *Made to Seem* (1995), *The Pretext* (2001), and *Veil: New and Selected Poems* (2001). Her writing, as Robert Creeley has described it, is one of a "clarity of syntax," with an interest in "the calm solidness of words"; but beneath this seemingly transparent presentation of the southern California landscape, with its metaphors of film, history, and popular culture, is a wry sense of wit (in both its meanings of droll humor and wise knowing). The poetry is also aphoristic and proverbial in a way that reveals the influence of American literary figures such as Gertrude Stein and Williams. Her significance as a contemporary poet is apparent in the collection of essays on her work, *A Wild Salience: The Writings of Rae Armantrout,* with pieces by Lyn Hejinian, Robert Creeley, Fanny Howe, Ron Silliman, and others.

She lives in San Diego, where she teaches literature and poetry workshops at the University of California, San Diego. She has also been the organizer of a poetry reading series at the university. With Fanny Howe she organized the highly respected "Page Mother's" conference on woman's writing at the university in 1998. In 2004 Wesleyan University Press published her most recent poetry, *Up to Speed*.

BOOKS OF POETRY:

Extremities (Berkeley, California: The Figures, 1978); *The Invention of Hunger* (Berkeley: Tuumba, 1979); *Precedence* (Providence: Burning Deck, 1985); *Necromance* (Los Angeles: Sun & Moon Press, 1991); *Couverture* [in French] (Rayaumont, France: Les Cahiers de Royaumont, 1991); *Made to Seem* (Los Angeles: Sun & Moon Press, 1995); *Writing the Plot About Sets* (Tucson: Chax Press, 1998); *The Pretext* (Los Angeles: Green Integer, 2001); *Veil: New and Selected Poems* (Middletown, Connecticut: Wesleyan University Press, 2001); *Up to Speed* (Middletown, Connecticut: Wesleyan University Press, 2004)

Range

There cloud moves in front of cloud, and above, suggesting
a deep breath, enormous range—such that a young girl
could leave home.

Long wind. Birds splutter and croak.
The difference now, she explains, is that she does not
lose consciousness when another takes the floor.

Who felt the vertigo of bouncing when he saw the fly
land on the leaf?

Who said, "Unnatural?"

The actress—the nun—the kid—the gatekeeper.

One harps continually
because she may have missed her cue.

"One notion, recognizable, with temperment and bluster
for real."

(from *Necromance*, 1991)

The Book

There's a fly
holding its course, manfully,
several long seconds,
stolid as the old Buick.

I didn't jerk back
fast enough this time
and now I seem

to know what's coming next

as well as I do
my own mother
holding up the picture book.
This is the world

of objects, faking
an interest in their own affairs
long enough for me
(the child on the logo)

to feel comfortable,
staring

(from *Necromance*, 1991)

Crossing

1

We'll be careful.

Repression informs us
that this is not our father.

We distinguish
to penetrate.

We grow and grow,

fields of lilies,
cold funnels.

2

According to legend
Mom
sustains the universe
by yelling
"Stay there
where it's safe"
when every star
wants to run home
to her.

Now every single star
knows
she wants only
what's best
and winks steadily
to show it will obey,
and this winking
feels like the middle
of an interesting story.

This is where
our history begins.
Well, perhaps not
history, but we do
feel ourselves preceded.
(Homeostasis
means effortlessly
pursuing someone
who is just
disappearing.)

3

Now here it is
slowed down
by the introduction
of nouns.

Eastwood, Wayne
and Bogart:

faces
on a wall in Yuma
constitute
the force required
to resurrect
a sense of place.

(Hunger fits
like a bonnet
now, something
to distinguish.)

4

On the spot, our son
prefaced resorption, saying,

"You know how we're a lot alike..."

He couldn't go out
on that day, but
he could have a pickle.
Out of spite, he crawled
to the kitchen, demonstrating
the mechanics of desire.

5

The sky darkened
then. It seemed
like the wrong end
of a weak simile.
That was what shocked us.
None of our cries
had been heard,
but his was.
When something has happened
once, you might say
it's happened, "once and
for all." That's what
symbols mean
and why they're used
to cover up envy.

(from *Made to Seem*, 1995)

The Known

The cat sniffs the bookshelf, and her knowledge of
its smell is punctuated then by a gingerly present
tense, relatively more acute, I guess, as time is
than eternity.

There is something stately about it. To ring is
stately. I am someone and everyone has something
solemn to tell me. One of us has died. I say I didn't
know her well—which is what I always say.

A dog's bark whooshes by, looming large on the night-
time or suddenly anonymous street. I could be disqualified
for writing, "suddenly"—or could have been "if the
truth were known" It's the job of the poem to find
homes for all these noises.

(from *Made to Seem*, 1995)

Turn of Events

Outside it was the same as before, scrawny palms and oleanders, their long leaves, ostensible fingers, not pointing, but tumbling in place—plants someone might call exotic if anybody called—and the same birds and hours, presumably, slipping in and out of view. She kept coming out onto the porch with the sense that there was some-thing to it. Perpetuation and stasis. She wanted to deal with the basics—though what this scene might be the basis for she didn't know.

This was her native tongue, slipping in and out of order—its empty streets and loose, flapping leaves, its bald-faced simplicity as if a way had been cleared for something huge. Shape was the only evidence. She went back in. She should think about how the house was built or how it was paid for. How a feeling can have a shape for so long, say an oblong, with sun falling in a series of rhomboids on its wooden strips. It would have an orientation. She wondered whether there was much difference between orientation and reason. She would sit facing the door.

(from *Made to Seem*, 1995)

Birthmark: The Pretext

You want something; that's the pretext. I recently
abandoned a dream narrative called "Mark." You
can see it, since you asked.

MARK

    I'm with three friends.
    We've parked in a lot downtown,
    lucky to get a slot.

    My son's friend
    asks him if he's divided
    his homework in three parts;
    luckily he has.

    Suddenly, I'm the teacher.
    I see a line of Milton's.
    I'm glad I haven't marked it wrong;
    at first I thought it didn't fit.

That's not very interesting or it's only interesting because it's real.
It's a real dream composed of three banal vignettes in which the same
elements appear: luck, parts, and fit. It's interesting to the extent that the
divisions and the fitting together arise spontaneously, without pretext. In
other words, to the extent that there is a stranger in my head arranging things
for me. Of course, I divided the *poem* in three parts. I chose the word *lucky*.

I have a real birthmark: a large red one on my outer left thigh. When I was
a child, my mother referred to it as a "strawberry mark," with seeming affection.
Was that some kind of trick? Because of what she called it, the mark has
never troubled me.

I didn't mind having small breasts either, though in that case there *were*
negative terms attached. Flatchested, etc. But gender is the birthmark which
has bothered me. When I was a child, Marilyn Monroe was the Sex Queen.

I know people feel kindly toward "Marilyn," but I saw something horrific in her act. Brilliantly horrific, maybe. She turned a magnifying glass on the problem. Those unwieldy bosoms held together by the weak "spaghetti straps." Tee-hee. Something was inadequate. The squeaky little girl voice would never to be able to articulate all that matter. No mind could get around it. So she would be a stranger to herself (and what could be more embarrassing or exciting)? Was someone ever lucky! We watched her pretend to pretend to be transfixed in the highbeams of our little girl stare. Funny how you can be excited without fitting in anywhere. But I've gone on a tangent when what I wanted to do was swallow my own pretext.

(from *The Pretext*, 2001)

Here

1

I'm here to recreate
the "fleeting impression"
that others once saw themselves

as repositories of experience.
In a dream
I'm three old actors

known for playing in Westerns.
We're on a trek through wild country
to show how the past might have been.

A voice-over says that our saddles
are especially worn and rough-hewn.

2

It's supposed to beautiful
to repeat a motif
in another medium.

A regular
dither
in the strings

approaching Apollo
Cremation. Out front,
fountains

make a statement
about the ability
to keep up one's end.

There's a boy down the street,
firing caps
as my son did

while a church plays
its booming
recording of chimes.

(from *The Pretext,* 2001)

Theories

Bird calls rise
and drop
to an unseen floor.

The son pretends
to slip
and falls

into a wading
pool,

limbs frozen
akimbo,
eyes locked

on mother.
One person

stutters as a way of
insisting
on unconditional love

and one who hears
a busy signal
may ring again

in anger.
What if one pretends

to restrain another
while the other

seems
to rotate helplessly

faster
and faster?

Each finds
his mate pre-

dictable

but believes his own
rigidity

must excite
his partner

(from *Veil: New and Selected Poems*, 2001)

As We're Told

At the start, something must be arbitrarily excluded.
The saline solution. Call it an apple. Call this a test
or a joke. From now on, apple will mean arbitrary
choice or "at random." Any fence maintains the other
side is "without form." When we're thrown out, it's onto
the lap of our parent. Later, though, Mother puts
the apple into Snow White's hand,
and then it's poison!

(from *Veil: New and Selected Poems*, 2001)

Veil

The doll told me
to exist.

It said, "Hypnotize yourself."

It said time would be
transfixed.

*

Now the optimist

sees an oak
shiver

and a girl whiz by
on a bicycle

with a sense of pleasurable
suspense.

She budgets herself
with leafy

prestidigitation.

I too
am a segmentalist.

                              *

But I've dropped
more than an armful

of groceries or books

downstairs
into a train station.

An acquaintance says
she colors her hair

so people will help her
when this happens.

To refute her argument,
I must wake up

and remember my hair's
already dyed.

*

As a mentalist,
I must suffer

lapses

then repeat myself
in a blind trial.

I must write
punchlines only I
can hear

and only after
I've passed on

(from *Veil: New and Selected Poems,* 2001)

Thérèse Bachand [USA]
1953

Born in Oakland, California, Bachand grew up in a large family of seven children. Her father, of French-Canadian extraction, was an attorney and, later, a municipal judge. Her mother, a school-teacher, kept close ties with friends living in a near-by convent.

Bachand attended Cowell College in Santa Cruz, California, where she studied with Norman O. Brown and was awarded a Bachelor's degree with honors. She moved to Marin in 1975, where she worked, first, as a housecleaner, and, later, as conti-nuity and camera reports technician on the film *Black Stallion*. From 1979-1982, whe was Marcia Lucas' personal assistant, doing interior design and household management. In 1983, Bachand and her family moved to the Los Angeles area, where her primary focus was raising their two girls. As her daughters matriculated through school, Bachand worked in various volunteer positions at both the Seeds University Elementary School and Marlborough High School. In 1996, she also worked as a volunteer at the Venice, California-based literary arts center, Beyond Baroque. From 1996-2000, Bachand was an intern copyeditor and proofreader at Sun & Moon Press, and later, Green Integer.

Throughout these years, she wrote poetry and involved herself in the local poetry scenes. But only after her involvement with publishing did she begin, reluctantly, to show her writing to others. *luce a cavallo* received the Green Integer's Gertrude Stein Award for 2005, selected by Luigi Ballerini. In this work, which characterizes much of her writing to date, the structure is determined, in part, by various movies from the mid-1960s to mid-1970s, a period which the author describes as creating exciting director-oriented works, that ironically have been cred-ited with saving the studio system. Others of her unpublished work includes a project using the daily newspaper as means to create a common palette of words, and *His Dusky Twin*, which is excerpted here. Bachand has published in several literary journals.

BOOKS OF POETRY

luce a cavallo (Los Angeles: Green Integer, 2005)

notarized assignation   (from *Accattone*)

what is the epitaph
for both
martyr and pimp?

a congregation
of a thousand pharaohs
arguing
abut the gentle sex
could not demean
such a free citizen

in God's hands
playing cards
becomes a honeymoon
for the lucky
a bashful reminder
that there is larceny
in heaven

the ravines
of the forgotten
brim
with working delinquents
petty crooks
who recognize
deceit begins
in hunger

let the countess
despise the grocer
robbed
of his false teeth

in this category
a holy medal
is but a necklace

a monument
in the shining roof
over the would-be
canonized-
those orphaned
by absent charity

(from *luce e cavallo,* 2005)

doll face   (from *Alphaville*)

the oral
is complex
spread Oceanic
through a tired room
of Bibles
prudence
is a whore
who believes in
the durability
of a bath
is alive to
the cinerama
of second class
for my part
I am suspended
in the furthest zone
beyond the orbit
of receptions and festivals
just as a newspaper
can arrange
a living population
into a tomb
the statue reclines
in a costume
of past centuries
technocracy

may self-destruct
but memory still
is the primordial custodian
of reincarnation

I cry
to be infinite
in this exterior country
but it is the privilege
of the dead
to be free
of absence

all
is consequence
a galaxy
can arrange electricity
while a sphinx
occupies
a district
of tomorrows
yet my tendency
to dwell in the past
transforms suppression
into a spectacle
of antimatter
a weapon
against fatality
to love you
a dictionary must
beguile the fatigued
"to sleep
perchance to dream"

to metamorphose
            into a poet
    having breakfast

            the sublime
        has a history
                of mutation
        I wander
            a labyrinth
    of the simultaneously
                closer

(from *luce e cavallo,* 2005)

ephemeral vérité   (from *Belle de Jour*)

A secret love can be the perfect coldness
unsettling any anniversary by forgetting to forgive.

A magician cannot understand the softness of snow
or the hypnotist's beautiful by unfortunate obsession with hunting.

Better to be underground in the cheerful and shy
profession of smoke and perfume,
awaiting fresh expenses and the matter of hello.

Close the curtain.

Money is the man's job
as is savoring ham & sausage,
a good pair of legs.

I like to have a good time
beyond champagne and pouting.

My temperature rumors
the dark and classy,
the fair game upstairs.

Death contrives homework that grieves lilies,
that accepts the closed door of a letter,
the scratching expiation of friendship.

(My unborn son is blonde.
He was struck by jasmine,
is clueless to my address,
his identity.)

(from *luce e cavallo,* 2005)

the monastery of one name   (from *The Color of Pomegranates*)

beautiful me
it is the soul's torture
that heaven and earth
are made in God's image

as the butterfly is abandoned in a cocoon
the ignorant are castigated by kind thoughts
for the benefit of their souls

the trepidations of a lyre
create breath in our searching selves
a refuge for what is dust
dead and suffering

my words are selfless
exuding aromas of innocence
devouring the inconsolable
while wrapped in fire

brothers, our immaculate flowers
are dressed in distant childhood
we have sacrificed the maidens
at the bathhouse of the weary troubadour

open the window
for the passing
of the swords

(from *luce e cavallo,* 2005)

Is joy
adequate?
As a postcard
can shimmer
with the still
of a squeezed headline
from Amsterdam:
"where the women sit
bored and all sexed up,"*
I feel
the make believe
of the skin princesses,
a boombox
a mantel, the
etiquette of glass,
the blurry weight
of an afterlife
cringing
on the shoulders
of what will happen;
for others,
what could.

*Phoebe Lithgow
postcard from Amsterdam, March 2003

(from *His Dusky Twin,* previously unpublished)

There is a design
for cursive writing
called the
gardenia law.
Full of swirls
and the insane smiling,
a tattooed mantra
of a mute arcade.

Every scientist knows
the syllables
exceed the syntax
on every nagging facsimile
of the poslished and true.

Anxiety is said to subtract
through hard work
what is yours = possession of the parts,
at best, a knowledge of
what falls apart.

(from *His Dusky Twin,* previously unpublished)

"her long quiet hands"

from George Oppen, Mary

keeper of melody
\<you\>
hum
not a junkie
to tune
but rarely re/
                    pressed

under glitter of dress-up
<you>
are not surprised
by my suitcase
the long sidewalk
charred by spectacle
of sunset

<you>
obey
your "long quiet hands"
the female equipoise
of home
the endangered and secret
plans of furniture
tones of refrigerator wire

(from *His Dusky Twin*, previously unpublished)

PERMISSIONS

Todd Baron [USA]
1956

Born in Hollywood, Todd Baron was a child actor, performing in movies, television, and voice-overs, for twelve years. He attended Immaculate Heart College for two years, studying with Martha Ronk, and later—focusing on contemporary poetics—with Peter Levitt. In 1984 he moved to San Francisco, studying at New College with various California poets, including Robert Duncan, Michael Palmer, Lyn Hejinian, and Diane DiPrima. He earned his Master's degree in poetics in 1989, returning to live in Los Angeles.

Earlier, Baron edited a journal, *ISSUE* (1982-1986) with Tosh Berman, and when that journal ceased, he began *Re*Map* (1989-2001). With Dennis Phillips, Martha Ronk and Paul Vangelisti, he co-founded Littoral books in 1991, a press that developed out of these poets' relationships with Lee Hickman. In 1997 he and Noah De Lissovy ran a poetics reading series at Otis Art Institute (now Otis College of Art). Over the past few years he has written art criticism for various journals, including *Artnews, Art Issues,* and *New Art Examiner.*

Baron taught at the Otis Art Institute, Los Angeles City College, and West Los Angeles College. For the past eight years, he has taught at the Crosssroads School for the Arts and Sciences in Santa Monica. He also continues to work with film, serving as a literary consultant to Klasky Csupo animation studios.

Although clearly influenced by his various teachers along the way, particularly in connection with their relations to "Language" poetry, Baron's writing is often centered on a fluidity of movement in line and meaning strongly influenced by film.

BOOKS OF POETRY

partials (San Francisco: e.g. press, 1985); *Return of the World* (Berkeley: O Books 1998); *(this...seasonal journal) (...)* (Providence: Paradigm Press, 1990); *Outside* (Bolinas, California: Avenue B Books, 1995); *Tell* (Norman, Oklahoma: texture press, 1995); *That Looks at One and Speaks* (San Diego: Factory School Books, 2001); *TV Eye* (Phoenix: Chax Books, 2003).

from *"the rooms"*

something there that comes,
that comments on or will,
                    there by itself, grammar
        of the field, field anywhere taken
    where voice is fact of air, now that
seasons come over the bridge,   a man
    woman or child, the act of stating "that's it," or
    That is it.   sitting & reading, call it
        Out on the Playing Field, a ball
    held tightly by rope, the wrist, red, upper portions
        of the plate,
                        place is a black substance, a rest
    not a glottal, memory coherent with time
        taken from him, linked to sleep &
    language taken in seams, not by breath, a cool'd longing

(from *Return of the World,* 1988)

from *"the rooms"*

I want to write, and writing, write.
                    so in the effusion,
        deems, willow'd, branched,
        comes a day. and there,
            here she says,
        moving in unmoving ways, chords so tight you fall be-
        loved, into & out of
    pitch-syllable.   poverty of glance
                    trees by a pin hole, someone coming
        takes this back from where it came,
    the text & the text, for texture,
        in tents not in caves, so in the final sense
        are other's language.   book on the table
        cup in the mask,

sun sticks in a circle of fire,
first rock or orb I thought would covet thee.   that I could love
blood flukes, despair & unbelief, that 'til my spirit
rises, they raise.   sit, stare
sighted, open in summer, to park, stare
or place.

(from *Return to the World,* 1988)

(series of three)

1

what is it, without image, metaphor, or doubt—

summer comes as fall approaches,
unstead and distressed *to see.*

voices hold
as leaves drop

chained to circumstance, brown
flora & other marks whose name

the sound of a chair, wakes
the middle of day, scrawling

sound of the bed, the floor, *bereft*
of nobility. the dream

in a dreamer's dream, coming
in a room, bored with reason,

even with reasoning. even the want
of need, & back again, a like-

geometry. a game, counting
windows by the road,

sitting on the deck, what passes for
silence as if it were a figure

gesturing the hand. bearing
each hand back towards

likenesses of imagery, old
father, older father, apprentice-

ship of facts, walking, waking
appearances of land.

2

what is this interior motivation—

to be given strength for everything
that blends into one. the vast

empty desert,
endless &

flooded with waters. like a movement shoehow
exapnding on rocks, that utterance

bordering the field. or is it
entrapment I meant to find

how beautiful and delicate, even
fragile, the framed

sad head was. A statue
a running set of monologues,

gripless and fortunate, wavering
indecision like a mask amid tracing elements.

the period the flower
of uneven questions asked.

uneven borrowed stares
of the irradiataed risk.

3

is it moments, out of place, *there's dust on the floor*—

the particular means of a particular shape.
is it morning & the fall and rising of sheets,

drapes, not the window or cars going by
outside the door. or the motion of sleep

as a statement of health, a statement of words,
of necessity. a problem of gaining, to

augment the self the untouched key
remembers. this, then in being,

taken reluctantly, fullest brightest scale
trying to reach the flattest modality.

searching uncertainty even
rain unfolds, even rain

encumbers.

(from *Tell*, 1995)

transparency

he wanted the experience back & into
the narrow regions the music

telling & from the distance toward he fixture
the camera moving clapping

a breeze the weather moving & a sound distinct
rain or a street a circumference

where the travels would each
& after sleep only

turning the ankles knees locked as if an arrow
losing a bend the entirety of silence

a light wind changing after a changing frost
a declarative moment the sound of a bell

to own is each an image picked ripe and found
in a jar a shelf of sand

a line over & about velocity & a list of things corrected
surrounding the pitch of day the rock

like a sound in the mind centuries overcome
by the significance of a phrase

"bouquet of roses in sunset" metaphor the real
emergence of colors the dusk brown hue

here in the morning after the harmonies have left
which is ever constant adversity like a fountain

made in the mist of the fountain the stream
fashioned in the sense of a stream in the light alone

the abundance of inactivity
the tangle of mass

(from *Outside*, 1995)

from "*(INDEX)*"

C

there's only an outside that comes from the inside
how many takes it takes to fill the lens

Placed and permeating capacity composition discerns control
when you count one who drew the course

or moved constellations afloat
a chain or chair a seat the ground until the edge

together to shake or form one mass
or clipping of stone "a single life"

a cell a hut to hide in
the strive against to stand corrode

Who made the track by signing addition
to avail a censor

originally a critic an opinion
not a contract rending throats

which merely means to talk to get it down
to where inaction was which merely means together and apart

across the other other
Coined from steel both

chapters unafraid the clouds are
charcoal vapor variations covered with cloth

A clump of citizens' senses
a bulb or sphere stopped

to drag
without them & entrusted

(from *Outside*, 1995)

from "*(INDEX)*"

W

there's only an outside that comes from the inside
comes a narration rending what happens to be

The secret eternity weakness serenity's calm
soaking the breeze

The sound of the drifter
reading desolate isolation wintering

tales of sudden unlit figures
resting the faculty

he said that she says writes
what she writes he says

the real who
unmystified forced to get out among branches

passes a building thinking belief
teped isolation blinding the page

overcome with himself he
who writes it is

unfinished work
labors   cultivation

learning the letter's pronounced
with only one tongue

only the thought
the remnant of time

(from *Outside,* 1995)

2
.

                    when you say (what
I think you say, that you prefer the
ordinarily immersed transcendental line,
what do you mean? For me
there is a secret to each
unraveling (like) film
moving an audience from one
matrix to the other . starting out to find
the "why of it" seems to generate
silence . (a squirrel
jumping from one tree,
the maximum of force
from which all things deliver.

I've known this conversation before,
and it's ours, meaning
yours, mine and his, but I also love
The smell & feel of the sun
on the balcony over the backyard
in the morning . waking
is constantly unattended, as if feeling
would rouse the day
as ciphers do, to find
a page that reads

each metamorphosis is there
when you're ready.

entering what appears to be a long trance
or just sleeping too late even knowing
that the painting in the next room
is really a clock & the clock
over the fireplace an object
found on the street, shy
of what comes as intention
or judgment.

outside the alphabet of each stone,
the idea abducted by loss
& the meaning of loss . the question of mis-
representation as a color of skin
or speech as the suns' reflected
by trees & the artifice of buildings.

as a footnote then
the form of an apparent journal
by less caustic remarks . but the
remainder stays the same
because a voice
is common & prosaic
to the question of vanity
& number . (the gardener cuts

grass & the smell
the scarcity of change . no,
there must be presence to time
as if it were devotion.

Buddhists meditate
on death.

                                        to *Martha Ronk*

(from *That Looks at One and Speaks,* 2001)

3
.

                        so you add to each day
a monstrous figure undressed
or undressing each state
with less heart than mind,
an outline of spirit, feeling
& growth . (pineapple sage in a pot
by the window, direct & laconic,
wanting the sun.

ideas & associations trace the subject of art
& the problem of light . reading old letters,
abstract & real, gone &
foreshadowed.

the mind as part of the body responds to distinct imagery

trying to break things down.
because it is singular
in the world, sentiment

& disfigurement, caring &
the opposite of fiction . (like aloe
outdoors, what manner
is redundant, what
motive regurgitates sound?

isolation respects the concept
of life, drunk or drinking
each doorway . my sense
of a house is one that's
unnumbered, equally
held & unbroken . that night
we sat by the stairs,
thinking of parallel visions.

tender, beneficent favors,
water boiling (kindly
generous meanings . limbs still
carry the sail no matter how
avarice or self-centered
waking is . but does that change
the music of change?
rather, watch each fire
as sleep modifies
each pronoun's response
to a place that seemingly
has no concept behind
or in front of—

one judgment, one logic
or symbol addressed.

to *Lee Hickman*

(from *That Looks at One and Speaks,* 2001)

Guy Bennett [USA]
1960

Guy Bennett was born in Los Angeles, but grew up in the suburb of Gardena. As a young child, his father left the family, and Bennett and his younger brother—a sickly child who died at the early age of 29—were raised by his mother and grandmother, both of whom spoke a dialect of Italian, the grand-mother's native language. In the late 1980s and early 1990s Bennett attended the University of California and received his Bachelor's and Master's degrees. In 1993, he graduated from that institution with a PhD in French literature. His interest in Futurism also led him to master Russian and Italian.

Soon after graduation, Bennett met Douglas Messerli at an Italian Futurist conference, and—after showing the publisher some translations he had done of Marinetti, for which he had recreated the original typefaces—came to work as typographer for Sun & Moon Press. Simultaneously, Bennett taught French language and literature at UCLA and other local community colleges. He also began to translate books from French and other languages, many of which were published by Sun & Moon and Green Integer. Previous to the publication of his first book of poetry, *Last Words,* Bennett began his own press, Seeing Eye Books (in 1997) which continues to publish four books, available by subscription, annually.

In 1999 he became Associate Professor of Liberal Studies and Communication at Otis College of Art & Design. The year before he married French scholar and writer Béatrice Mousli, and together they now split their time between Los Angeles and her native Paris.

In 2000, Bennett published *The Row,* and in 2001 his chapbook 100 *Famous Views* was published by 108.93 press. The Italian publishing house ML & NLF published a bilingual collection of his poems, *Drive to Cluster* (with art by Ron Giffin), in 2003.

Bennett has continued to translate and to typeset books for several local and national publishers. With Standard Schaefer, Bruno Franklin and Chris Reiner, he organized a poetry reading series at a local café. And he has been active in several poetic ventures throughout the city. With his wife, Bennett organized an exhibit and conference on "French and American Poetry in Translation" at the University of Southern California, the Autry Museum, and Otis College of Art & Design in 2003.

Bennett's writing, like his personality, is witty, urbane, and highly focused. His writing often has formal systems quietly embedded in it, but the poetry itself in influenced by a wide range of interests: music (for several years he played bass in a local musical group), photography, film, architecture, and, as one might expect, the languages and literatures of other countries.

BOOKS OF POETRY:

Last Words (Los Angeles: Sun & Moon Press, 1998); *The Row* (Los Angeles: Seeing Eye Books, 2000); *One Hundred Famous Views* (Atlanta: 108.93, 2001); *Drive to Cluster* (Piacenza, Italy: ML & NLF, 2003)

Terms, unused anticipations
that progress delusion,
omitting conscience
regarded as feeling
that process makes knowledge.
    Their treatment,
after touch taken inward,
contrasts the interest of our views,
the unfit cry of things,
the common sense.
    For orthodox leisure needs reason
as ceremony corrupts dialogue,
achievement and confidence suffer,
and acts appropriate circumstances,
wanting code beyond code.
    The creature-fed
contradition fallacy
of wisdom wrestling concern
suggests external is best—
a spirit separate to man.
    Arc capacities without life
a question answered?
—Things sense
the good required,
their proverb secret.

(from *Last Words*, 1998)

Distances accumulate fictions.

A dissolute mouth admits
solutions that quake in beat.
    That beautiful desertion
holds loose expression,
becoming a skill of language,
a lateral land that retains
the sea.

(from *Last Words,* 1998)

In immediate entering.

        That putting,
        the first time,
        that situation.
Being already first from age,
        having life,
        been others,
        being defined
        when happening,
        when though,
        when young.
        But in other instances
        of setting at time
a being got crazed and occurred,
        when what after
        valued enough
        the virtue
        of seeing,

(from *Last Words,* 1998)

Puffing like midgets, life's weary train
—beyond going—too hope,
its proud blinders longing to fail.

Forgotten, then suddenly adrift,
it shunned tight dust tumbled up in cups,
trembled lightly to shower motifs
and the shuddering echo of homeopaths.

All around, lighter time flutters, then bellows.
It tells us when one word is still enough.

(from *Last Words,* 1998)

Clock the real.

Twice glimpsed
precisely, / leaps
invert each mood,
their effects
leave nothing
but matched becoming
and prolonged
air. / Retractable,
the discretion of
increasing distance
a ceiling
to open monument,
back of
since, / the
head deciphering recoil,
the evasion
its touch
explodes, / an instant

striking the
second / when
at present, / you
hadn't an
hour of
thinking a return.

(from *Last Words,* 1998)

What thinks resists.

Light—precisely light,
    it ideas ourself,
collecting memories,
digging up and imagining
the night.
    We who know point,
handcuffed to the radio
of outrageous self-indulgence.
    Others,
Insensitive to long grass,
chirp the scream—
an example of freedom.
    They consider
to consider reality
(still vague)
while we embellish
our very initial.
    We shimmer and fire,
a flaming bird.

(from *Last Words,* 1998)

The only road onward
is inward; so must sound go,
threading a pleat of voices
through the space
an idea can occupy.

This space expanded,
driving horizontal to the depth
of polyphony, reaching down,
compressing (compression
means expansion), breathing
new wind, writhing the light
of one hard thought.

(from *The Row*, 2000)

Everything is derived from one basic idea,
spun like thread through the eye to thought.

Its inner energy a resin a synergy sparks,
as scrape-walls round the open whole of the throat.

A question of composition, of form, the fracture
of stillness; perhaps the most important thing is this:

what sounds. Its abject resilience glints broad
the bow drawn over the arc of the strings.

Its elemental accidence of point of arrival,
spiritual to the blunt rebuttal of clutter.

Only on the basis of these unprecedented fetters
has complete freedom become possible.

(from *The Row*, 2000)

Sound sounds still stillness, the silence
we were before, breaking to say bridging, obeying,
then fitting off-dark thoughts to new shapes
perhaps more unlikely than one might think.

May this course sure the distancing our
inner eye already corners, clearly threading
the sheer shell from form-ideas, uncommoning
the sharp handles our said strings pulled?

It has been—this cause is all about what
we wish of stings we knew before them:
we ring them in, shard them simply to law,
now, an entirely opposite way down.

(from *The Row,* 2000)

Eight Architectural Miniatures

20858 Pacfic Coast Highway

This oceanside defined
brutalist balance traffic
blasts rhythms its bays
with motor access pediments
light: an infilled, level sandstone
wall of glass blocks touching
the antiquity-fine, shoreline
grid high as the sea,
an armature glazing
spaces flow-linked by light.

909 25th Street

The barrel-vaulted volume
hearts the bougainvillea grape
wisteria and trumpet run above
the house from the sun-square
skewed axis the street looks
oveer to the studio's open, green
                stucco trellising visual presence
                twist-breaks as bands of compact
                color space the lot-lathe light
                        shafts streaming between
                        the project's great gardens.

455 Upper Mesa Road

A hillwide view blocks tower
connects this home's steeply
sloping site to monolithic
sprawls' elegantly understated,
elevation-shaped volumes, cladding
plaster-wood copper and zinc-coated
layouts bedroooms bottom as loft
spaces curve to terrace
two room masters.

1955 1/2 Purdue Avenue

Earthquake pulses design
striking buildings, absorbing
devices base isolators
cylinder within viscous

substances, smaller units energy
efficiency panels and clad
the floor and walls steel
frames enclose inside
faces' exposed visible interior.

5905 Wilshire Boulevard

This pavilion-exuberant, idiosyncratic
Orientalism structues curving, tower-
clad, aggregate bridges the stairs
elevator as columns triangle bowed
box beams suspended from cable-pale,
green stucco curves organic "walls
evoke, paneling angles that face
the softly lit space a quiet ramp snakes.

940 North Mansfield

This sandwiched cement
works' west-towering
glimpse treasure troves props,
offering unexpected, truss-
eruptions of building-filled, blue-
curved structures shape-scattered
detritus makes sense of, as complex
sound lounges casting vaults'
exposed workspaces bridges
stair cross from place to place.

8687 Melrose Avenue

Built blue to house bright
forms, scale the surrounding,
              aroused, float-altered
          extension to contrasing
       fragments symmetrical green
          spandrels rotate away via a
plinth the skylit atrium's cylindrical
    hinge-curves wedge in red glass
    phases the plaza poured in place.

1641 Woods Drive

    Floating the city this
    house captures, 180 cave-
    like, completely glazed
views transform the steel
studded, sun-clad panels that
    glow night like space enclosing,
    frameless spiral climbs
              the mezzanine deck transluces
          from the copper dropped ceiling.

(published in *Place as Purpose: Poetry from the Western States*, 2002)

Franklin Bruno [USA]
1968

Born in Pomona, California in 1968, Franklin Bruno was from a family of Italian immigrants. All four of his grandparents had come from Italy, and both his grandfathers grew grapes and boysenberrys in the area. His father taught psychology at San Bernardino College, and wrote several textbooks and popular reference works.

Bruno received his Bachelor's degree in mathematics in 1990 from Pomona College, and a Master's degree from Claremont Graduate School. He is currently completing his Doctoral dissertation in philosophy at the University of California, Los Angeles. Although his philosophical training has primarily been within the Anglo-American tradition, he personally resists the notion of an unbridgeable gap between that tradition and Continental philosophy. At UCLA he has taught courses on property rights and symbolic logic.

Although Bruno describes himself as mostly self-taught with regard to poetry, he was influenced by courses at Pomona with Jed Rasula and Dick Barnes. He began writing seriously in the early 1990s, and published his first work in Paul Vangelisti's *Ribot* in 1995. He also participated as one of the writers contributing on a regular, monthly basis, to Vangelisti's *Lowghost*. Since that time, he has contributed to numerous journals, and has had one small collection published by Guy Bennett's Seeing Eye Books, *AM/FM* (1999). He has also completed a full-length collection, "Rhododactyl."

Other than poetry, Bruno is very active in music and music criticism. A guitarist, he has been the primary singer and songwriter for the rock trio, Nothing Painted Blue. The group has released four albums to date, and have another, *Taste the Flavor,* planned for 2004. He has also been involved with other recording artists such as Jenny Toomey and The Extra Glenns. Music criticism of his has appeared in the *Los Angeles Times, The Village Voice, Spin, Time Out New York,* and *CMJ Music Monthly.*

He describes his poetry as "arranged" or, preferably, "accumulated" rather than written. The work often deals with music and other elements of popular culture.

BOOKS OF POETRY

AM/FM (Los Angeles: Seeing Eye Books, 1999)

2

I'm not ready to go
to bed when you are
a top, beside me, restless.
I have used magic,
used rough music to get you
to hear my supplication
my one brief mission
before sleep, my implacable
voice vined with romance.
When you turn, I'm spun
gold on the wheel of your arms.
I've lost this thread
once already, and don't plan
to find it again, to keep track,
nor to listen to your spinning,
your whistling forever.

11.8.97

'carving nature at its joints'
        instead of outlining its cellular structure
a conclusion 'come to' like consciousness
        pure and tasteful, a black tower
absorbing the opportunity cost of
        common beauty, pillow over face
high harmony and tight rhythm
        shrillness of newly strung guitar
tone of an unfamiliar amplifier
        but how some black things shine
ritual: pursued vehicle spins out
        shatters on impact with big rig
delivery system for thorns and
        the boiling core of a private sun
99th time making the same list
        slice of body held in grip of theory
force, a cadence caught by the back

of the neck on an ampersand's hook
what's meant, then, by 'two parades'?

(from *AM/FM*, 1999)

5

project this conflict
into the ragged space between

action and reflection
static signal static signal static

cut away the lexicon
wherever it doesn't tell one's story

black paint worn green on café chairs
coffee in a cup-shaped coffee cup

crest trough crest trough crest
presence, absence, some third term

in a series of hollowpoint kisses
which mediate or oscillate between

the public testimonial
and the privacy of consolation

a mirror which captures
sound instead of light

"You're just around the corner from the place you met your love...."
"You think your life has changed for good, but then it changes back."

the newest radio
receives the oldest music

4.4.98

neither a gatekeeper
    nor a gatecrasher be
a skin pasted over the how
    and how many of circuitry
valley fold in the cardboard ocean
    clean design not evident
in finished building. This looks into
    fire for you okay. Hazardous
materials may include explosives,
    compressed gas, flammable liquids
and solids, oxidizers, poisons,
    corrosives and radioactive materials.
Fugue state in cut time
    I'm south of here where wading
in closed and gaudiness might
    whittle at what the supernatural
corrodes. The red sage
    a cigar box a cupid's bow
I'm north of here where unity grows tidy
    with corrugation, a shoulder knocked
onto the carpet tacks. I press stop
    stop presses, ring the hoping
bell of one eye's waiting

(from *AM/FM*, 1999)

8

the oldest radio
receives the newest music:

the money worries
the screen grabs

the field guides
the winter coats

the baud rates
the nerve gates

the streets here;
a map of a tree

the trees here;
a popup book against the horizon

an Ellsworth Kelly wedge of sky
visible from my doorway

a too-familiar poster
that functions as a window

bears its own resemblance to
the freight of reading

through too little light
and too much smoke

4.17.98

a state is what you alter
     a nation's what amasses
remarks aren't politics either
     everything that has a liver has a kidney
or isn't too easy to begin with
     given the century's hot raving, sharp knife
and me indexing disjunction by loose
     wires at the back of each security camera
not so many years ago, the African
     National Congress was officially considered
a terrorist organization by the CIA
     a ghost is glad for something pure
motion and surface fluttering by
     a boy in the smog, introductory
weather falls like irrefutable proof

(from *AM/FM*, 1999)

2.

(Z) The time at which the film is shown.
(Y) The time at which the film was made.
(X) The time of the represented events:
Quadrant defined by three orthogonal
axes in conceptual space, every
screen a point within it. Louis
Vuitton clerks attend night classes
in Japanese, so their commissions
might increase. Earlier, rose-
golden wisps of pancetta flavor
platter of squash. Chloroformed
kerchief blown back into Verdoux'
face: "I can win a lottery,
that's more than you can do."
Later, an acrostic *beau present*
'upon' the name of the alphabet,
 hooked into meaning like A-V
office-keys on trusted senior's
jeans. Earlier, in radio drama's
waning days, a fierce Raymond
Burr commands *Fort Laramie,*
ending what *Gunsmoke* began.
Now, when did the taming of the West
cease to seem a past
receivable as ours?
Depends on your accent.

(from "The Accordion Repertoire," *The New Review
   of Literature,* 2003)

5.

Tomato soup poured out
upon the waters, a piece of driftwood
enameled pink, so that its value
might increase. Disparity is right
around the corner. Transcription errors

infect Vivaldi midi-files. Earlier,
Gracie Allen calls Confucius
"That ancient coolie" an hour before
I drive to Echo Park to see an Asian–
American folksinger from Raleigh,
North Carolina: "Hey Hey Hey
record company
sign me up
before I go nuts." Later, leathery
man plays Cuban songs among
pluots and plumicots, Hollywood
Farmer's Market fills cruciform
space bounded by Ivar
and Selma. Earlier, a wop
longshoreman murders a scandie
lottery-winner: "You need-a the dough
to get-a the breaks." Later, Venetian
concierge in *Trouble in Paradise*
translates Edward Everett Horton's
lengthy plaint into one word:
"Tonsilia!" Earlier, plums
rot on the ground, so gold is
amassed for its very uselessness.
Later, eldest Foy relates "Little Red
 Riding Hood" in a working-class variant
of mid-Atlantic accent: "And then the wolf
tore both her arms off." Now
having rounded the horn
we return to civilization
the long way, as long as any account
of what's worth fighting for,
or fighting: "No tickee,
No kissee."

(from "The Accordion Repertoire," *The New Review
    of Literature,* 2003)

6.

Awe to, foe toe,
maw no, pie row
graph: Notation slows
the wheels of steel; tears
(a stain or a strain)
lubricate the gears
unseasonable rain
decides whether 'iron'
is one syllable or two
and whether 'rough'
to force or forge
a link with Tin
Pan Alley. I run?
I earn? Unreasonable,
sane. 'I' is for 'item.'
Got 'em? Light 'em.

(from "The Accordion Repertoire," *The New Review*
of Literature, 2003)

Wanda Coleman [USA]
1946

Born in the Watts community of Los Angeles, Coleman escaped a life as a welfare mother after the post 1965 rebellions by becoming involved in a number of social organizations designed, as she has put it, to channel "the riotous" energies of young Black Americans into constructive modes. She worked as a medical secretary, a magazine editor, a journalist and scriptwriter, all the while writing poetry and taking various creative writing courses, including a course with Clayton Eshelman.

She began publishing poems in the late 1970s, and published her first book, *Mad Dog Black Lady* with the famed Black Sparrow Press in 1979. From the beginning her work was deeply concerned with issues of racism, but over the years she has gradually transformed her work from a dramatic performative representation of inner city African Americans to a more experimental investigation of voice and the positing of the Black American. Although her influences include Black writers such as Phyllis Wheatley and Paul Laurence Dunbar, she also cites other writers such as Walt Whitman, Herman Melville, Edgar Allen Poe, Edna St. Vincent Millay and Emily Dickinson.

Among her many books of poetry, most published by Black Sparrow, are *Heavy Daughter Blues: Poems & Stories 1968-1986, African Sleeping Sickness, Hand Dance, Native in a Strange Land,* and *Mercurochrome.* She has also written short stories, longer fiction and memoir.

In 1999 she received the Lenore Marshall Poetry Prize. She has also been awarded grants and fellowships from the National Endowment for the Arts, the Guggenheim Foundation, and the California Arts Council

BOOKS OF POETRY

Mad Dog Black Lady (Santa Barbara, Black Sparrow Press, 1979); *Imagoes* (Santa Barbara: Black Sparrow Press, 1983); *Heavy Daughter Blues: Poems & Stories 1968-1986* (Santa Rosa: Black Sparrow Press, 1987); *The Dicksboro Hotel* (Santa Rosa: Black Sparrow Press, 1989); *African Sleeping Sickness: Stories & Poems* (Santa Rosa: Black Sparrow Press, 1990); *Hand Dance* (Santa Rosa: Black Sparrow Press, 1993); *American Sonnets (1-24)* (Milwaukee: Woodland Pattern/Light & Dust Press, 1994); *Native in a Strange Land: Trials & Tremors* (Santa Rosa: Black Sparrow Press, 1996); *Bathwater Wine* (Santa Rosa: Black Sparrow Press, 1998); *Mercurochrome: New Poems* (Santa Rosa: Black Sparrow Press, 2001); *Ostinato Vamps* (Pittsburgh: University of Pittsburgh Press, 2003)

from *American Sonnets*

12
—*after Robert Duncan*

my earliest dreams linger/wronged spirits
who will not rest/dusky crows astride
the sweetbriar seek to fly the
orchard's sky. is this the world i loved?
groves of perfect oranges and streets of stars
where the sad eyes of my youth
wander the atomic-age paradise

tasting

the blood of a stark and wounded puberty?
o what years ago? what rapture lost in white
heat of skin/walls that patina my heart's
despair? what fear disturbs my quiet
night's grazing? stampedes my soul?

o memory. i sweat the eternal weight of graves

(from *American Sonnets*, 1994)

17

i am seized with the desire to end

my breath in short spurts. shoulder pain
the world lengthens then contracts
(in deep water—my sudden swimming. the surface
breaks. thoughts leap. the Buick bends
a corner. an arc of light briefly sweeps the dark walls)
everywhere there are temples of stone
and strange chantings—ashes angels and dolls

i forget my lover. i want a stranger—
to shiver at the unfamiliar touch of the one
who has not yet touched me

a furred spider to entrap my hungers
in his silk. with virulent toxin
to numb my throat

(from *American Sonnets,* 1994)

Essay on Language (7)

snapping

a warped sense of communication
impairs the business of conventional narrative

like feeling robbed, the rules of orgasm no mystery

given a voice, one must struggle with one's own
social type-casting on the edge of ambiguity

it's exclusively inconclusive

(language cannot contain this magnitude of afro-agony.
righteous rage is difficult to keep jacketed)

snapping. not a march (on Washington or anywhere else),
but a death ballet

I am compelled to protest
the demise of the deliciously clandestine.
the new underground is sterile,
devoid of dangerous rhythms, and strewn
with the grotesque bones of riotous fists

drowned birds. thru the art
                    thru the art

(looks as desolate as a chassis graveyard)

repeated midnight embraces. yet i've slipped
out of the framework of love
lost confidence. all these years wasted.
no lucrative controversy on the literary horizon

(the centaur bends over me, towers. release
in the blade of his tongue)
issuing from the culture

one bullet and a nation bleeds for decades
speaking of dragging out a bad ending

what neither illuminates nor exemplifies/corrodes
grappling with onset of antipoetics
badly mangled intent and didactic syntax

alas. i may never find the proper adverb

snapping

(from *Mercurochrome*, 2001)

Incomplete Acts

hiding the face after it makes
front page news

straightening out a bent disposition

killer shadows armed with nasty gats
chasing down a rat on the eve of righteousness

wise & ultimate peace

squeezing the three-hundred pound lady
into the size ten life

rising out of the dungheap unstained

he looks the part. trying
to make him play it

finding a cure for October

(from *Mercurochrome,* 2001)

Espantalepsis (3)

winter my beloved

like our hair, our dreams are going gray
the stars are winking out
first a father, then a child, an uncle—and soon,
others, including a mother or two
who will be left to care or carry on?

a chill in the bowel

here we are divided from comfort by lies
and stubborn jealousies/the hateful manias
fed by ancient rivalries & misreadings
(who was most loved? who was punished or spanked
for every niggling mistake? who was deprived
of childhood? who most desperately seized the night?)

a dulling of the reflexes

there is no rescue. the larder
is full of moths. little white moths like
annoying flits of decay. there is no luck. chaos
steals our sleep, crisis robs us of time & cash

brittle nails & thoughts

hours crawl yet weeks fly
bones spit and curse bad steps
first slow then slower. light hurts.
strange noises confuse the ears. bruises
refuse to heal. the pose causes muscle strain

numbness & tingling

winter my beloved
nothing made of flesh is safe

(from *Mercurochrome,* 2001)

Against Forgetting Cento

and the crows go by…

my teacher revealed a pattern
a black shaft loomed up inside me and grew bigger
as night grew
yet i leave this earth a lowly eater
without having tasted good meat
in this neutered air where mad Nijinskys swoon
in ambidextrous ennui
better to have never been born than to die ignored

       mistress of slumber
       white sleep
       bloodfire (my breasts swollen and itchy
       with his suckings)

America, I broil in the racism which makes
me who i am—just another dead voice
without a booking agent

i have learned how women fall to bone
how true women suffer what false men celebrate

these ravings in my ear come off the yap
of a faithless friend

in this dark time brave tongues are mute
inthis field of cinders i am the smoke
my genius turned ferocity

i fall down on my knees and beg

my son's terrible eyes
my son's terrible eyes and sad cold hands

(from *Mercurochrome*, 2001)

Broken Rhythms

like spellstuff   all the conceits i have shed
collect   on sun-slashed soil   where a
three-headed woman gathers them to make
her hoodoo   a powder in fire   to summon a spirit
a finely ground pinch of alcohol   to cure
a cough, or in a salve   to beautify aging skin
make your wish   for love   for hate
and burn the fragrant wax with a hint of dust
chant   toward the sky   watch. the children gather
watch the children   dance   watching the children's eyes
watch.   the children with tongues   like wolves.

(from *Ostinato Vamps*, 2003)

Soul Traveler

not dispersing but containing blackness

it was the ending and so reruns began
Amazon style, summer came calling,
fried brains and all. dumbfounded
in Los Angeles where mosquitoes drowse
in noonday heat, bloodlust drained from
tropical eyes, the air thin as a haint's brassiere

luxmobiles took the heights like llamas
where dollars shine from foreheads as smooth
as polished fenders, and from oversized
designer pocketbooks toted under shaved
and flavored underarms, breasts revealed
in bright colors, tank tops and bustiers

negra Afro angel

pat those cheeks in Spanish,
those too round trotters—a lingo dug by all

quietly there's reciprocation in snatches
from whistling lips, sunbeams and posters of James Dean

(shy tourist girl, a face all acne and
inexperience, shares her mother's
private smile. "buy something, some trinket.
support the local economy")

the emissary of G.O.D. calls her over,
places the silver cross at her throat, fixes her
with agate eyes, fingers splayed against
her hips. she follows him to the other side
of the moon, counts the hours under azure,
feigns reaching for her pen

note: plastic trash bags, cheap jewelry, the ebony cat in the cradle

she is made of ocean spray,
condor feathers and memories of sin

(from *Ostinato Vamps,* 2003)

PERMISSIONS

"American Sonnets" 12 and 17
Reprinted from *American Sonnets* (1-24) (Milwaukee: Woodland Pattern/Light & Dust Press, 1994). ©1994 by Wanda Coleman. Reprinted by permission of the poet.

"Essay on Language (7)," "Incomplete Acts," "Espantelepsis (3)," and "Against Forgetting Cento"
Reprinted from *Mercurochrome: New Poems* (Santa Rosa: Black Sparrow Press, 2001). ©2001 by Wanda Coleman. Reprinted by permission of David Godine.

"Broken Rhythms" and "Soul Traveler"
Reprinted from *Ostinato Vamps* (Pittsburgh: University of Pittsburgh Press, 2003). ©2003 by Wanda Coleman. Reprinted by permission of University of Pittsburgh Press.

Robert Crosson [USA]
1929-2001

Born in Canonsburg, Pennsylvania in 1929, Robert Crosson remained in the East until his family moved to Pomona, California in 1944. He attended the University of California, Los Angeles, and received his B.A. in English in 1951, briefly joining the Communist Party during his college years. After college he began working as an actor in television and film, in 1954 landing a small role in *White Christmas.* The following year he appeared as the character Danny Marlowe in *I Cover the Underworld.* But Crosson grew increasingly dissatisfied with the Hollywood scene, which, combined with his brief political activities, dimmed his prospects for further Hollywood employment. In 1959 he traveled to Europe, working his way through various countries as a piano player, a black-marketeer, and pimp.

DOUGLAS MESSERLI

In 1960 he returned to the United States, enrolling in Library Science at the graduate level at the University of California, Los Angeles. Eventually he dropped out, taking night jobs and attempting by day to write his first novel. Jobs as a painter and carpenter, another movie role (in *Mike's Murder* in 1984), and a 1989 Poetry Fellowship from the California Arts Council, allowed him to survive during these lean years; however, as he grew older Crosson grew increasingly dependent on "the kindness of strangers" and friends, particularly Los Angeles poet Paul Vangelisti, who—when Crosson was evicted from the Laurel Canyon house where he was caretaker—took him in. Crosson lived with Vangelisti from 1993 until his death in 2001.

From the early 1980s to his death, he had several books of poetry published. He 1981, his first book, *Geographies,* was published by Vangelisti's and John McBride's Red Hill Press. They also published his poetry (along with the works of two other poets) in *Abandoned Latitudes* in 1983. *Calliope* was published the following year by the Los Angeles publisher Illuminati. In 1994 the Italian publisher Michele Lombardelli published Crosson's *The Blue Soprano;* and Guy Bennett's Seeing Eye Books published *In the Aethers of the Amazon: Poems* 1984-1997 in 1998. But most of Crosson's writing remained unpublished at the time of his death—the result of a heart attack brought on, doubtlessly, by years of heavy smoking and drinking. Luigi Ballerini's Agincourt press published *The Day Sam Goldwyn Stepped off the Train,* a selected poetry, in 2004.

During the last years of his life, Crosson was beloved by Los Angeles innovative writers for his eccentric behavior—he was gay and often described in some detail his sexual encounters and experiences to both his gay and straight friends—his unusual sense of humor, and his poetry, which came to be recognized as some of the most original writing of his peers.

BOOKS OF POETRY

Geographies (San Francisco: Red Hill Press, 1981); *Wet Check* in *Abandoned Latitudes: New Writing by 3 Los Angeles Poets—John Thomas, Robert Crosson and Paul Vangelisti* (San Francisco and Los Angeles: Invisible City, no. 3, 1983); *Calliope* (Los Angeles: Illuminati Press, 1988); *The Blue Soprano* (Castelvetro Piacentino, Italy: Michele Lombardelli editore, 1994); *In the Aethers of the Amazon: Poems* 1984-1997 (Los Angeles: Seeing Eye Books, 1997); *The Day Sam Goldwyn Stepped off the Train* (New York: Agincourt, 2004)

The Fastest Gun in the West

'My dear we have been here before'
two sides holding a doorknob
smarting a first dose of crabs
the dog human (as sheets go) 3$
extra to shower in rooms shared
the hollywood address
hirsuite (suite) palms
o yes that   on franklin avenue
catholic god
wits & witness
                              first it was captain marvel
                              encumbrances sunk the ship in
palm trees doheny   voices dittering offstage
before the sunset   'that horse cant be rode'
orange groves &   but by god I did it 5
hill barren   times around on my ass
free to be (bought)   the first take &
picture postcards   without glasses
                              caught the bag of gold

                              *

the story ws   coffee shop.
this a house a dog   this guy comes in
trying to get in
goblins geese   deaf jack from the old
losing weight make   boarding-house days 15
test of virility a   yrs since hes seen me
cornucopia of slick   'you still in the acting game?'
shells one goose   one night modeling a tiger-girl
a guinea hen   in suit jack takes picture with
                              his color Polaroid

                star to the territory

          catcalls (off) the
          proscenium arch
          snorting by-yr-leaves

                               *

        'global to be sure'

that moat & fortress
held drawbridge she
took back roads from
life (or film) held
terror to

'my dear we live here'

backstage lots
abandoned
properties

'extras are not people
      bits should associate with'

                *

you know the lamp over
that is good luck
one goose dead
& I open in
2 weeks.
today
i buried it

she sd i was a genius i
believed her i cd fly when
i wanted i could mount walls
verily and do

cyclopean steps
up the outside
rock amphitheater

    *

guns are for people to shoot with
i found that out when i was in the
war guns are heroes & guns make
heroes stronger i stand for that
guns are war, can warn off the
gas company or mad dogs up the hill
say coyotes

       tin targets of an evening
when I am john wayne & intend to be

      * * * *

listen i have a very good vocabulary to tell you
the truth i can screw you without yr knowing it
& love you for it i am no star-fucker that is a
lie i ws put on this stage to say god made me
special i ws born with it you can keep philosophy
ill take shakespeare theater is my life it runs
in the family

* * *

i am very loving
until someone shoots my guinea hen
or turns out to be a drunk i do not
like drunks they fuck up i speak
from experience the real man walks
in his own boots i do not drink or
smoke i am a vegetarian.

so i ws born with a silver spooon
call me a playboy in this life
you use everything you have

       im running aboard ship
       the total holocaust i
       did my own stuntwork
       (scale) 'in water this

deep and no wet check

'horses i can handle
but that

           the supply clerk
celebrated home during
the mud slide
george sand

telling about gray rains
in mallorca the piano
peasants so troublesome

'got medals to prove it'

                    *

i don't doubt it
given half the chance
id shoot the sonsabitches down myself

a sure draw from the hip (target
that guitar hanging poolside)
and take the fuckers in 6 fast shots
like that
12 blocks south of the company store
yr legs thumping
to run a fast bum check

                    *

           star shop
           picture postcards

           okay so i ws captain marvel
           i was also batman & wore a cape
           i still have, wear boxingmitts
           with my sanadrock padded dummy-bag
           my goat stands audience

fuck the neighbors
i am my own man my mother made me
i demand the best that is tickets
paid for this is war to yr friend
be faithful i did not
strangle my wife

        *

she just lost her brother
she is a champion skater
she can hit hard she ripped
the doorjamb off & threatened
the hinges that is some lady
(she also painted my bedroom silver)
i asked her which brother she ws calling
'the dead one,' she sd

thats on my telephone bill

(from *Wet Check,* 1983)

Letter

   The christian name makes impossible
   any face-front exchange of plain talk.
   The remedy (as I've sd before) runs
   amok the chittering squirrels on roof-
   tops & owls (tail-balanced) hung from
   trees. Adjectives kill, or stultify
   and, in any case, belabor the room
   we so carefully establish. Privacy
   hs everything to do with it–topical–
   and them day-old sausages brought (un-
   wanted) to the door we eat anyway,
   threshold and lintel.

You tell me we have five years to
change the language. I wonder what
you mean. Me? Us? Why? And what's
to change? Maybe you didn't say
'change the language' but we hd 5
years. My overalls will be washed
fifteen times by then, some shredded
for lawn chairs; the rest abused &
at least one pair given my dentist
as collateral...Poetic endowments
(? To be sure) get me in fistfights
at parking lots.

(from *Wet Check,* 1983)

The Hartford

–can't remember his name: a distinguished
writer; friend of a Friend who'd once played
tennis with his daughter–his house, a splendid
quarters off Doheny... I was invited guest.
His wife, much younger, went out for a swim.
We shared drinks.

"Trouble at The Foundation," he informed me,
was "Too many 'pansies'–; glanced at the
 manuscript it had taken four years to write–
read the fist page. "Well," he said, "at
least you're literate."
They had a dog–

Just down the street from Stravinsky

(who'd already left.

(from *The Blue Soprano,* 1994)

Coffee Table

–meant read the right magazines.
Made prominent.
Didn't matter if you had one.
That was protocol.

Somebodys-wife who wrote for The New York Review–
Special reservations held party,
before bed.

———

He sat atop me.

I was thinking of the organist
in Allentown.

(from *The Blue Soprano*, 1994)

Brecht

Boomie wrote me letters–
he kept copies

He had a sister and a brother-in-law.
His step-sister was a film star whom
I never met. She was mistress of Howard Hughes.
Nights, she would sometime visit the family.

His father (deceased) had once played the violin.

———

Very camp-gossipy letters
I have lost them.

Boomie was a director.
He knew Elsa: we once spent weekend at the
Laughton peacock-Farm in Palos Verdes.

Elsa (inimitably) maintained that spices should
be put with the pasta, not the suace.
She like watching car-races on TV.

(from *The Blue Soprano*, 1994)

Lemon

The lover I never dreamed of wouldn't speak
When I was at the ocean too.
Seaweed and salt and wind
Blew every list away.

Words that would make me laugh now
Snorted bulls and boardwalks
Me. Me. Coins with the head of Ceasar.
Flapping seagulls.
And.

Under a log, left worms and white.
White–until I'm blue in the face.
The mirror lit.

Candles. Or stars
Cut to the bone.

Toenails and chairs and elevators.
Faces in back seats. Wet skin.
A corked bottle. Salt
And seaweed.

The bare word he said
Needed dead men.

A green car.
Gone to the moon.
All thumbs and fingers.

(from *The Day Sam Goldwyn Stepped off the Train,* 2004)

The Red Onion

A charley-horse was not an erection, but a cramp
in the leg. Men whistled walking by the house. I
didn't much notice it needed painting.

    It was a red house, barn red. One side of it was boarded up, I never went in there. I imagined it ghostly. I sometimes thought the men were whistling at me. But it was not the case. The house was wooden, a very old house. I lived with my aunt, who rented the upstairs. Nights, I tried to imagine what it would look like, but I could not do much with it. The yard was a mud shambles: nothing could grow there. I could not imagine it a new house, nor did I want to. It was not in the right place.
    The reason it was called The Red Onion was not what I thought. I thought it was called that because it was red–though a red onion is not red, it is purple. I did not like the men whistling when they walked by. I pretended I didn't live there.

(from *The Day Sam Goldwyn Stepped off the Train,* 2004)

The Man in the Moon

In this bright-red-paper wading boots,
His well-worn thumbs–:
'You must be drunker than I thought!'
      And dove into the lake.
          —PATCHEN

The way the water shows the hills.

A milky rim–an edge
To this naked guy:
Head-first.

A husky fellow, ready–
No sound of splashing; nor
Penetration

Moon.
A still-like–

Rock-reflection of
What's plummeted.

(from *The Day Sam Goldwyn Stepped off the Train*, 2004)

Pythagoras

Evil resounds like water.

Water is a way to think.
Thoughts drink well at noon.

Four is tonic and more fertile.
Five is sometimes marriage–
Sacred to Aphrodite.

Stark failures of the drowned.
Misery like success is infantile–
Feminine, wanting both yes and no.

Seven is the mind–virgin, musical–
Associated with the birth of heroes.
Eight seeks eros, ultimate friendship.
Unburnished.

Water reads like skin–
Numbers sound like dance running.

What comes next, a question in the mind.
Half dozen of the other–
The first perfect number.

Moons incarnate.

Hand in a pale of rum so far from June
it makes one want to dance–
June, an alibi

For myopia & romance.

(from *The Day Sam Goldwyn Stepped off the Train*, 2004)

The Collar

I feel like I'm wearing a watch:
The hand to the cuff–the Ballpark–
Colorful folk stealing each others' cars
And suits of clothes they live in (after
Retrieval) or bets on the races:
A world of bookies and fast laughs.

The sacred, sacred.

How to nail your hand to a board and drive
Timber to Emergency: how to lose a finger
And (again) pick up the guitar or piano.
How to walk crossroads against the light
And make it fine kettle of fish, having
Lost the sportspage or pooltable left
the backdoor open, or the wife
At her embroidery.

A round-trip to Aussie-land where babies
Are borne to pouches and eat Kiwi–
Aborigines prowling in the bush
This side marbled architecture they
Haven't shoes to fit: the fix of a smile.
Celebrating.

A child hugging his mother's skirts.
Where sea is that and stone is a place
Of choirs.

(previously unpublished)

Catherine Daly [USA]
1967

Born in Decatur, Illinois, Catherine Daly grew up in the small town life of the Midwest, the daughter of a commercial real estate broker. Her mother worked as an interior designer, and her younger sister later became the Director of Fundraising for the Sundance organization. Daly was valedictorian of her class in her Catholic high school, and went on to receive a Bachelor's degree at Trinity College in Hartford, Connecticut (1988), and a Master of Fine Arts at Columbia University in New York (1991). From 1984-1988, during her Trinity years, she also worked as a disk jockey, and later, publicity director and program director for the radio station WRTC.
After graduation from Columbia, she worked as the recording secretary for the CIO office of Bankers Trust Company. From 1996 on she moved to Southern California, becoming an independent technology consultant for various organizations, including The World Bank and Boeing Groups.

Over the next few years, she would also begin to teach writing and poetry courses at the Los Angeles Community College District, UCLA Extension Program, and Antioch College. Simultaneously, she continued to write poetry and reviewed extensively in such journals as the *Kirkus Reviews, Rain Taxi, American Letters & Commentary, The Boston Review, American Book Review* and *Poetry International.* She also wrote numerous essays for independent and academic journals. Throughout the early 2,000s, she curated various literary arts festivals and a reading series at the University of California, Los Angeles's Hammer Museum. She also read her own poetry extensively, resulting, in part, in the publication of her first book, *DaDaDa* by the United Kingdom/Australian-based press, Salt Publishing.

Daly's poetry reveals the influences of both her technical expertise, expressed in her consulting work, and her Catholic education.

BOOKS OF POETRY

DaDaDa (Cambridge, United Kingdom/Applecross, Australia: Salt, 2003); *Locket* (Hartford, Connecticut: Tupelo Press, 2004)

LCD / LUCID / LEWD
from "Palm Anthology"

Resonance boosts amplitude.
Do you identify
palm with hand, tropics
with tropes and ropes?

Sparks jump from your skin
to my skin
or spark pattern anywhere
like a Catherine wheel –

you could see
me, and I you,
and touch.

(from *DaDaDa*, 2003)

Ice
from "Oos"

I, mine, shine belief in
their belief in thine.

I desire nothing within sinners.
I anticpate, reminisce, worship.

First conception,
during passion–tribulation's expiry–disposed,
precarious, building, family.

Fluid-dipped, dripping.
In height, prime, zenith, epitome.

Despoiled, despoiled attire,
hidden in peculiar finery,
veiled,

cranium hit with sticks, crimson with violations
immutable, inexpressible.

Pit recognized against lineated,
illuminate disguise.
Implore
anamnesis:

nothing
encompassing limits imprisons
this universe in mine.

Nails,
first nail, pain within pain,
cite
dislocating
carrion,
remain.

Distinct figure,
into fists, confide
being
inchoerent.

Medic, medic
pain like thine,
–continuous–
gains liberty.
Passion is
promise
with mine
in Paradise.

Darling,
divested, *Girl, view this heir.*

Luscious knife-edged animation,
relieve inexhaustible origin.
I thirst.
Inflame desire. Extinguish it.
Spirit, enlighten delight,
this twining vine, universe, wine.
Precious majority, wail *pourquoi*
cherish *quoi?*

Point, line;
dive. Immersed
instruct purity in
affection's habit.

Mirror, tissue, tie,
limitless, innumerable multitude is thine integument.
Darling, again?

Inscribe
ventricles with vital juices, signs.
I will examine adversity,
aggrieve Mediation.

If it transpires, receive
passion's litany.

(from *DaDaDa,* 2003)

Listen

MARGARET(H)A EBNER

My sister was like the police. Serve and protect.
We raised no controversy. We lived quietly.
My conscience was free. We never submitted.
Bound by law, we acted according to our consciences.

Sick we suffered and patiently endured pain.
I saw she would die. I would have died for her.
When ill, I was unkind. She didn't hold that against me.
I was with her until she died.
I thought I could not be without her.
I saw her once in a clear vision while I slept.
She consoled me. I can't write it.

I was asked to write, just begin and write whatever.
I feared and dreaded writing.
I wanted
to act
according to His will and obey
the man who asked me to write.

While I wrote this little book,
the sweetest grace came upon me concerning Jesus' childhood.
I have a stature of the child in the manger.
Delight attracted me to it.
I took the image out of the crib and placed it against my naked heart.
I perceived power in the presence.

Out of depths I cried out
for some authentic sign
he came like a friend after matins.

(from "Heresey," *DaDaDa*, 2003)

Woman and Island

TERESA DE CARTAGENA

My life's borders carry me
to an island where I live, if this is life.
No one showed me any community of pleasures.

More sepulchre than dwelling, this island
is my dwelling.
It can't be populated–

who would forego temporal pleasures?—
I populate it with consolation.

I hear neither good nor bad counsel.
I recur to my books.

Deafness cut me off from distractions
and removed my desire. In company, I am forsaken.

What good is speech?
Speech is pointless without hearing.

Language can praise and preach.
I can praise and preach without reply. I write.

Do not think suffering overlooks a great mind.
However learned or quick-witted, sense
can't help me.

Without hearing or speech, my intellect
I exercise for myself
without writing. Illness
safeguards from occasion.

My judgment neither proves nor demonstrates.
My limited faculty and the few years I attended the University of Salamanca
make me responsible for the simplicity of what I say,
grant me no wisdom in what I want to say.

Men and women marvel at my book,
a brief, slight work. My offense is clear.
Their awe results not from my text's merits
but from its author's defects. Some can't believe I wrote it.

Some marvel a woman can write a book.
No one marvels if men write.

I had no master nor consulted with authorities
nor translated from other books,
as some say.

Knowledge alone consoled me,
alone read me.

(from "Heresey," *DaDaDa*, 2003)

The Curious, Pervious St. Catherine

Light, road, word
permeate her porous dictée, her doctrine,
which, under the purview of deviant popes,
she deviously disguised–

what god quotes himself–

as mnemonic device.
Purloined principles buttress her beatific bridge
and tears.

Perhaps that signifies her perviousness,
a perquisite if not a prerequisite for her hidden stigmata,
not perverted but pure.

(from *DaDaDa*, 2003)

PERMISSIONS

"LCD/Lucid/Lewd," "Ice," "Listen," "Woman and Island," and "The Curious, Pervious St. Catherine"
Reprinted from *DaDaDa* (Cambridge, United Kingdom: Salt, 2003). Copyright ©2003 by Catherine Daly. Reprinted by permission of Salt.

Michael Davidson [USA]
1944

Born in Oakland, California on December 18, 1944, Michael Davidson attending San Francisco State College and continued with graduate degrees at The State University of New York at Buffalo. He is currently Professor of English at the University of California, San Diego in La Jolla.

   Davidson began publishing poetry in 1972 with *Exchanges* and continued throughout of 1970s with three further titles—*Two Views of Pears, The Mutabilities,* and *Summer Letters.* In the 1980s he published four new books of poetry—*Discovering Motion, The Prose of Fact,* and *The Landing of Rochambeau,* and *Analogy of the Ion*—as well as

publishing a critical studies, *The San Francisco Renaissance: Poetics and Community at Mid-Century,* and, more recently, *Ghostlier Demarcations: Modern Poetry and the Material World* (University of California Press, 1997) and *Guys Like Us: Citing Masculinity in Cold War Poetics* (University of Chicago Press, 2003). He also was the editor of *The New Collected Poems of George Oppen.* A trip to the then Soviet Union in the late 1980s resulted in a book of prose (written with Lyn Hejinian, Barrett Watten, and Ron Silliman). Beginning in the 1990s, he published two further collections of poetry, *Post Hoc* (1990) and *The Arcades* (2002).

BOOKS OF POETRY

Exchanges (Los Angeles: Prose and Verses Press, 1972); *Two Views of Pears* (Berkeley: Sand Dollar, 1973); *The Mutabilities* (Berkeley: Sand Dollar, 1976); *Summer Letters* (Los Angeles: Black Sparrow, 1977); *Grill Work* (Toronto: Mansfield Book Mart, 1979); *Discovering Motion* (Berkeley: Little Dinosaur, 1980); *The Prose of Fact* (Berkeley: The Figures, 1981); *The Landing of Rochambeau* (Providence, Rhode Island: Burning Deck, 1985); *Analogy of the Ion* (Great Barrington, Massachusetts: The Figures, 1988); *Post Hoc* (Bolinas, California: Avenue B, 1990); *The Arcades* (Oakland, California: O Books, 2002)

The Waking

It is never over,
a rain awakes him
repainting sleep, anticipations
of a cloudless day;

what alterations of a weather
alter the sexual air,
that brings these leaves
later to replace the flower,

and somewhere in memory
to replace themselves
with space? He waits
to reconstruct a dream:

a room full of people
watching t.v.,
a movie of people
who are watching t.v.,

so that an end is never over
but down there
down a perilous track
or tracking shot

and on all sides
the heavy metal screws and bolts
fall to be arrested
just in time;

the natural tower
forms a limit to the tale
that holds a field
of folk telling

who move in and out of movies,
roads and rolling hills,

who have a part
in great designs,

whose faces illustrate
this rolling globe in space
that seems
to stand upright

like a man following
a dream,
"a dungeon there-inne
With depe dyches and derke;"

he sinks back
and works the edges of rain
into a sea or plain,
a screen fruitful and grey,

it was a tale he knew
from Chandler or Hammett,
a cenotaph for the missing child
they'd stolen

in everyone's distraction,
it was about places
returned to in the night,
the rain beating down

so sanctified the way
a field seen in youth
becomes blood
bone and liver of a later sight;

he was stolen to protect him
from endless regenerations
of the mundane view
of self on screen on self,

it was clear
they had no purpose,

like the rain they played
to work him open-eyed,

music of this ceaseless war
erecting monuments,
burning towers to modulate
ever downwards in sleep;

he saw the way the woman
moved among the notes,
her breasts and thighs
almost present but turned

into a landscape
about to yield,
the plum and apple blossom
pressed to glass

and mixed with rain;
she was a presence of the end
he'd never see and so
this music seemed to be

an early opus, "Il
Cimento dell'Armonia
e dell' Inventione"
to trick the walls

and send them tumbling
back in place
to where they'd always been,
a harmony of all distracting

sun, it shines
even in the marrow
where the waking takes its shape
among the dead.

(from *The Mutabilities*, 1976)

Concrete Example

White fishing boat on thin strip of blue
seen above green fence on any day
but today is important
because it coincides with this
"concrete example"
in which the importance of history
must be sustained
in the face of the facts,
"the facts"
are on sale in any small country
dependent on us for aid, and "us"
is whoever believes them,
the fishing boat achieves a trajectory
of self-interest in variable space,
all it has left
is its wake.

(from *The Prose of Fact*, 1981)

The Philosophy of Composition

The palms wave at 4:14
and again at 4:30
as part of the wallpaper effect
of certain afternoons

in the south, the anxieties
of Winter give way
to the sweet yearnings
of Spring, all right

the same old anxieties
the point being
you thought the seasons
exerted their "local" effect

when it was *you* all along
and your nervous tic
that gave the air the air
of a Wallace Stevens title

while inside,
lapis lazuli, opus six,
Eurydice and her mirror, ruins
of Piranesi, the Mad Trist

of Launcelot Canning
which you just made up
to explain the French
who invented Poe, Summer

extends its tentacular reason
from beyond these fictions or maybe
these gem hard truths
of finger, arpeggio, telephone book

which should remind you
of how this all started, the palm
at the end of April
finally reaching you.

(from *The Prose of Fact*, 1981)

Paranoia, The Doppelgänger of Hemophilia

The very large world in the form of a room. Something leaks onto the floor that con-
cerns you. The amount of time it takes to refuse a newspaper salesman. Slowly,
something from the past refers to you. What you must have looked like during the
Civil War. Something seeps out, gets absorbed. It is not quite history but it is not
quite sign either. The birds, at this hour, taking advantage of a hollow hour. What
you can safely do during it: Bogart as a test pilot bails out according to some unfin-
ished business. A documentary on divorce. An interview with a famous author.
Basically I just love my mother. I was an ordinary child living in an average large

house. Some small river that is you, yet not yourself; something that expresses you. In this sense I am not alone, only bookish. Having to keep the parts at a determined angle, reading straight ahead or not lying on the left side. He found a body decomposing that had not been intended for his eyes. Armed with Joyce and Oedipus, she solves a number of academic crimes. Something that became a clue, a dark spot spreading. They are as near as the phone; they sail far and wide, farther than you could see. They have their lives, after all. The mockingbird imitating the duck down the street: demon or bird, the word most delicious.

(from *The Landing of Rochambeau,* 1985)

Post Hoc

When the bell rings twelve times
the grid begins; at the end of the grid
a punctuation and before long
action becomes possible

the word for action is delay
this way a point bleeds into the fabric
until it is revealed as a face
and the name of the face

will bring people to the fence
when a picture bleeds
he is not in time but time
is what you call it

then they will bring you money
and the bell has done its office
the body
permits you to leave the body

(from *Post Hoc,* 1990)

Hypothesis

I began
scattered
recollected in parts of the city
the parts that remain useful

rusted shed
mossy creek bottom
deserted produce district
narrative begins

in friable youth
loses itself
in uncomfortable consonants
gh and cc, water

is an ancient hypothesis
earth floats upon it
"like a piece of wood
or other flotsam"

in my second book
the censor permits us
to see everything
I refuse rehabilitation

and leave with parents
for the beach, sand looms
large in a life made up
of the opinions of others

for with dispersion
we become compound
and take on the protective coloring
the desert demands

blue heron which is grey
great egret against green pine
grebe that ducks for crustacean
in dispersion water sounds

like everything else
a crowd of mocking boys
in the balcony and film
about an ape and a helpless girl

injustice begins
in the way they tell the story
of my story
I am a monkey that coincides

with a small organ, in the telling
I happens
discovered among cattails
forbidden words

or the olfactory richness
of basements, something indistinguishable
from something else
is handed around under the table

(from *Post Hoc,* 1990)

Gentrification

Seek remedies in the sleep margin
uncited men drinking and slouching
in transitional downtown, one
dances along a pediment on the second floor
another watches
to be in their threadbare
there must be electronic gadgets

in the open air arcades, portable remedies
in the parking corridor
where the corner meets
another corner, accounts anticipate
these consumers in the big ledger
injections of an otherwise effluent
of a profitable share, the blimp
is a rentable vantage from which a pitched
ball becomes a Ford
while a struck glare and bombed basement
disappear from the front page
inconsequential as a mental recently released,
read these as an imperative attaches
to luxury and the intersections
will suggest themselves
much as a city creates signage
to give access to access.

(from *The Arcades,* 1998)

Translation

Against the black sea of a black night
a single light
of the duty free shop, blazing
on a broadcast horizon;
all the drowned sailors
are restored by its siren;

Deseret changes; old neighborhoods
are an allegory one steps through,
the predictable and repeated windows
filled with the glass of novelty
that by wearing becomes new
as a pilgrim arrives refreshed in Jerusalem;

I think of you, hapless shopper
stepping through mirrors with a map of Troy
only to find yourself
frozen in representation like a swan
in Audubon, dead sweaters
roam the aisles searching for lost husbands;

Within the cloacal streets of the old city
that gather like phlegm in the throat
new boulevards form in the mind
of a white architect nearing the end
of a life spent
among the dark consonants, the mass;

We would be signs
dragging once snowy plumage
through ravaged construction sites
that progress raise visible portions of itself
to explain the benefits of speed
the violet frisson of acceleration;

Where was Africa?
someone in an office of tusks
on the fourteenth floor asks
and in the absence of palms and musk
a museum of masks retains these black
distances behind protective glass;

In the aisles of exile
I think of forgotten sailors
who search the horizon for a solid thing
when wings are signs of harbor
frozen like script in azure
and bring back junk for the stalls.

(from *The Arcades*, 1998)

Leland Hickman [USA]
1934-1991

Leland Hickman was born on September 15, 1934 in Santa Barbara, California. He moved with his family to Bakersfield, living on a farm in Carpinteria, and, ultimately returned to Santa Barbara where he attended high school. In addition to acting in high school plays, Hickman performed in local theater productions of the Children's Theatre of Santa Barbara and the Group L Theater Workshop. After high school, Hickman attended the University of California at Santa Barbara, and later studied at Berkeley, where he performed with the Berkeley Drama Guild.

Drawing by ROBIN PALANKER

After a tour in the Army, Hickman moved to New York City to continue his theater career. He toured nationally with the Bishop's Company in 1957, worked in the Canal-Fulton Summer Theater in Ohio in the summer of 1958, and performed with the Equity Library Theatre in New York. Subsequently, he studied at the New York Academy of the American Shakespeare Festival.

In 1961 he returned to California, performing at the Equity Library Theatre West in Los Angeles. He remained in Los Angeles for three years, returning to New York. But in 1969, He moved to Los Angeles—briefly living in San Francisco—where he and his companion, Charles Macaulay, lived the rest of their lives.

His literary career began in the mid 1960s. In 1967, *The Hudson Review* published "Lee Sr. Falls to the Floor," an introductory poem to Hickman's major work, *Tiresias,* his "ongoing long-poem" about his feelings for mankind, poetics, and America. He continued to write poetry through the 1970s, publishing a section of *Tiresias* as *Great Slave Lake* Suite in 1980. Portions of the work also appeared in numerous magazines and anthologies throughout this period. His work, highly narrative, might almost be seen as a sort of western, mythologized version of Walt Whitman's work.

From 1977 to 1981 (issues nine to eighteen), Hickman worked as the poetry editor for the Los Angeles literary magazine, *Bachy,* published by Papa Bach Bookstore. In 1981, he co-founded, with Paul Vangelisti, the magazine *Boxcar: A Magazine of the Arts,* two issues of which were published. In 1985, he began editing and publishing *Temblor,* which continued for ten issues. This magazine, one of the most important of its day, is noted for the publication of national figures, particularly those connected with "Language" writing, and international poets. Throughout these years, Hickman also worked intensely with local established and emerging poets, questioning and challenging their poetic values and methods. Accordingly, he became an influential figure within the southern California poetic community, one who would apprise his peers' works honestly, tolerating little self-satisfaction and personal eccentricities in their writing.

In 1991 Hickman died of AIDS.

BOOKS OF POETRY

Great Slave Lake Suite (Tieresias I:9:B) (Santa Monica, California: Momentum Press, 1980); *Lee Sr Falls to the Floor* (Los Angeles: Jahbone Press, 1991).

Anaximander

In the final nites of the Infinite,
when out of the sleeping sea,
            the prickly-skinned crawl,
generation will dry their days
And after their skins
            break off them,
they will love for a little while

In the final nites of the Infinite,
wherefrom all things conceivable spring,
the fish will change
            into the man
the bear will change
            into the man
the spider, mouse, antelope
all living things
            will change
into the prickly skin of man,
there to live for a little while
And the sun will raise new vapors
lifted by the Infinite
            into new living things
thrust into the sleeping sea
to float there,
            until their final nite

But what shall we do,
            Diogenes,
when the wheel refuses to turn again,
when all of our stars are stopped up,
and when finally the sea
            is completely dry?

[1956]

(from *Lee Sr Falls to the Floor,* 1991)

Lee Sr Falls to the Floor

his breathing unthrobs

Rerun that   The fumes
Tremble in the terrifying heat
Lee Sr falls to the floor

Rerun that   Lee Sr crumples
angular on linoleum
gasps in the kitchen glare

Rerun   Lee Sr falls down
in jockey shorts   A wooden
chair topples on its side   smacks
the floor   back goes
his balding head   clawed
by ache

        Rerun the gasp

Rerun these inchings thru
instantaneous reruns with
a feel to the eyes of
unfocused imagery

Rerun that   Lee Sr crumples.
dead. In the bed   down
the halflit hall
his greyveined mistress
sleeps out of life whose
fleshings creamed his dark.
The boy her grandson falls
in the hallway   hands gripped
to the urgent splitting of
time away   his pajamas
drenched with the wet
of fire quenching fire   They're
dead   and so the fumes

have no more purpose   no
effect   effected
by agents out of time
who do not know the job is
done   who never despair
never tire   never quit

Gasp in the kitchen's glare
in the halflit sweating hall
the deadly fumes   Speak from eyes
ears taste touch gut:

                              Rerun all

this: the fumes rise
as nearsighted Clifford
peers thru deathsprinkled glass
raps   shatters the glass
trembling at the hot
voom of decayed breath
And walks thru the dark
living room rapidly   no
rerun that   inches thru
the black toward the
flame of the heater   no
paralyzed   coughs   waits.
afraid to move utterly.
toward the light from the hall.
slashed across the floor.
squinting Clifford.
afraid to move utterly.

Rerun! Instanteneously
dashes toward the light
sees peripherally someone still
in a shadowed bed
down the lungdamp hall—
stilled creamdark fleshings
whose images fumed and flamed—

hurries thru the hall over
the dead boy   peers
thru the kitchen's glare   sees
one bare foot gelid blue.

'I am a tiny child'
whimper the words in him
as the floor slides back
as the boy dies
whose death it is
as he sweats for the warm
still halfseen someone.

      We take a greyhound bus,
      we run to an angry dad.

      Rerun that   We go home

              Cliff
stoops to lift the broken
chair and slumps down   staring
at a hole in the brown linoleum, near
his father's bent bare
unfocused image
fixed in fleshings as
creamy blue and as stiff as
two days dead and never before
beaded with sweat like this final sweat

And now rerun
the gasp the ache the urgent
splitting the stumbling fall
the toppling chair the
quitting the rapping the
rapping the breaking glass and
the personages as
flickering stills the
personages muffled   I
hang up   I tell my brother John   We board

a greyhound bus   We
go home   holding our
breaths in fear
that our breaths will vanish
claimed by an angry god

No, rerun that   We go home:
We just / go home.

[1965]

(from *Lee Sr Falls to the Floor,* 1991)

Hay River
For Henry Urbanosky

Husht
squalid like my dad in a grave in my brain, burial of
        verve, blind dumb deaf wet grovel dis-
stances clampt gag & my mindfold tight on me can't
breathe or die Hank & I all my scraggled song dumpt go
        battered out of night toward Great Slave
Lake this bus rattles over gravel ruts flat long dirt
forest road north one dark & a thin dark day under far-
        off lightning & gray nervous
boreal rainfall my writhen corpse who is me before me
        moans o for me o for me o to destroy me

& once my son dying

once my son dying late prayer dream I'm 9 years old in our old
        black jalopy   my dad
dead, dead in the front-seat in a black
        overcoat   my mom
        invisible   drive us

to my movies in my night-
time not on any road but high up, out
        in my sky where meteors
        shine thru her I lean
forward   between them my baby my son his gaze his gaze
        sunk time in my night-
time daddy daddy he's dying my dad wakes up to
touch the tip of a finger to my baby's
chest I whimper I wail out loud my december
        gusts sting in thru
        busted out windows my tattered up-
holstery flaps crazy in wind
                              stream my teeth
chattery hey what theayter we goin at what movie what
        movie we gunnasee once we git there see the glow
        from my laughy live son late prayer dream
light my frozen dashboard my whole jalopy fiery how we blaze clear, clear
        out here in my wilderness   onward   onward

wilderness onward onward I'd die to
        go into that forest & never come out what did
        you say Hank says I say I
said I'd die to hide in this forest/I see her in a sudden
drizzly clearing   visions you ache for & ache you, they
gnaw rake wrench split you & carve you in they gnaw, stock-
        still, torn skirt bleak sweater boots &
gusty about her in mazy twilight her dying eyelids lift
        toward the downrush glide
        of the solitary
raven swooping deep into wet glittery aspen shadows she holds
armload of dampt kindling whitehaired Slave Indian crone & children
        run past here into the hut with kindling
& the rain, whispery upon her somber face she burns
rigid toward gray over ancient glade my bus roars by I
twist in my seat to see her buried under branches how they
        thicken between us & cover her,
        how I cover her here in my interior
grave her gaze motionless toward gray her raven winging within me
        thru rain spray chill in last

pure wonder & now: Hay River, Old Town, on this cold
  southern shore

toward cold southern shore, forest dusky
  trails muddy, icy
  scud, low sunrays slat I listen for
  source sound enfold guide me to my-
self, hide me in the, at first far-off frail
  moan in my spine, Hank
leads on running soon spruce & aspen thunder the
  rumbling en-
  gulfs me some-
thing beyond convulsive suffers seethes
  rages in itself, Hank
  bolts forward, breaks
  thru my final
  trees I am pulled, skulled
thru my wrencht Woven-Here down stark hard sand Great Slave
  Lake's gnarled uprushing roar
shudders daemonic its groan thru me my night sun-
  light gleams blood-rust on my waves, gleams
off floating tree-hulks far out adrift sinking &
  heaved huge black in
slow moiling cry wind squalls sand, leaves, over weatherbleacht tree-
  trunks washed up on
shore ragged roots flare gaunt against lightning I gaze I gaze
  long into my night how lost my light goes

(from *Great Slave Lake Suite,* 1980)

The Hidden

For Harry E. Northrup

o   law I die
under nothing to do with free
kind my brutish
law, out
law miracle, crawl, sweat, to glory, got
adventure & got ascared, dad, dad, my dad, a
version, blue eyes under silt by sea not light not light not
work on what has been spoild nor furthers
my work on what has been spoild   o

o   all the poets are Hidden. stoned
occlusion bursts into word-rain, dad songs
me high thru my blue sun breath door I cry I
cry war my jews my japs die, dad at canal red shoulder white
thigh, hate
him, tell, tell, re-tell, how the time's
hard, oat slabs
float in the lard, dad, grit in the kids' swiss
chard, stink bugs
fart in the yard   o

o   to nothing, no not
to nothing to
this this is this, what
alone my lone this is, great beyond
lazy wild sky in my fingertip, right ring
buried bunkbed splinter dad gouges my blood of nightly, for
me, & licks for me speechless, dis-
figured flesh-sign worried with a needle o, how many sun
downs dad got us down we awestruck divine we go to? I sing
this yr one poor gift for lack of one better my scar my gully
& way-gone 34 orbits later, tell   re-tell   o

o   this is no
saxophone solo dad but I can sing I can make it
all, yr frycook cuss wingspan riveter teethsuck flat times flat

broke ball-peen clawhammer crosscut bevel, level,
plane, make it all & yr odd sharp stare past me thru
lost Bakersfield Calif shack sunbeam dust,
past forsook Nebraska farther back alone dad I can make it all
well, with my tremolo learnt in school sweet & high
to yr sapphire birthstone beltbuckle knuckles long blond eye
lashes clear up there on a peace   ful sum   mers eve   ning when
the sun   HAS   set don't bury me with you dad don't
bury me with you don't   o

o   & jagged from lockheed   & bitter   hisses
belt out of belt loops   lashes ass often   how I
must cringe   hate   breathe in in
secret   grow nervous ecstatic Hidden   set fire
to ladybugs   weep   hurt fat girls   weep   seek boys to
scorn me   dig in my dark my shovel snaps breast
bones   & how out loud wd I shout it   shout it out
fierce   whip me dad whip me whip me til he crumples   & caves
in   in me   whimpers Sonny   scat far you to task what lights
of yr catechisms   whip you   task barren
trees   barren skies   whip you   task any
sad   wrong   old   road   beat you & wail
all yr poets Hidden son I nail my breath door tight & still   o

o   one blond slim 1949 dad's one solid stunnnd
noonburnd carpenter on his own poor man's plumbd
redwood rooftop beveld & groind against one gruff song
from our longwinded sky in a glare under far blue sun
who stonefaced stares down at a boy
skinny & scribbling at the wheel of the stalld black jalopy those harsh
hardond mystical clear
groans got forgotten whose unclear
glance flashes breathtaken high
into his breathtaking higher up enemy's eye & both do remember
that ocean in their brains where it rains forever. only as long
as one quick flare wch fire flings slick down his naked spine
that the man wrenches back to hammer & shinglestack,
& the boy in the black wreck falls back to his fresh black song   o

o   & crablike out of navel brung into dad crab
lice son snuck off to yr queers again? & pours
acrid brown lark
spur on my balls, dis-
gusted plucks at my armpits sideburns eyebrows ass w/mom's
voice at the door last damn straw damn last damn straw & at dawn
this salt-fog hides my house where's my
mom, gone, son, gone, for
good & curses his wall as I cling to their fog-
lit doorknob, their pillows flung to their cold
floor, their sweatwrencht sheets clamming to his thighs as he
smokes, coughs, stub burns small &
soft gray ashes fall on his white bare toes, dis-
gusted I watch him curl in his head & breathe in slow we swirl
quiet & alone under thick low fog swirl   o

o   then as tho strangling, retting,
each day more taciturn, dad
after she left him, the one
decade left him, trappt, in far worse sours than child stuff, roots
determining, so that even as he had at 15, his, dad, I had at 16 also
left him, as even
his angers left him, leaving
some tenderness &, as he told me,
an ache for one only he narrowed his heat to, held to,
put it in the work, son, put it in the work,
& a day came, all of his sons having left him,
& his daughter much more her mother's,
that I saw him standing still in that crowd of dead children, staring
heavy into the low flame of himself, & alone, like a stranger   o

o   nine two twelve, twelve four sixty. dad per-
haps wakes, his woman asleep, her grandson asleep, his head
aches, rises, dizzy, kitchen, lightswitch, coffee his head
ache retch blur boy hall fall help crash cup hand crash
chair & falls & falls & falls fumes & eyelids not any
air monoxide flutter like that. fast. silence. or dad perhaps
bolts out of dream-shriek, temples exploding, & the
woman beside him, dead, the boy in the hallway,

dead, dashes, kitchen ache chair stumble crash slips retch
hand doorknob fall, fall, immediate night, dawn, noon, twilight,
night, dawn, noon, ringings, knockings, young man hollers, anybody,
nine, two, twelve, home? twelve, four, sixty, anybody,
dawn, dusk, dark, home? in all that dark? in all that dark?   o

o   for the entire process is benign, don't
bury me with you dad don't, on a hill top, view of
Pacific, placed coffin, & I descended to it, work on what has been
spoild, & knelt beside him, entire process benign, raised
my left arm, one finger toward sky, rested my right on
his silence, go in to my Hidden, earth rose around me, process
benign, passing thru blue sun breath door, shut it on
panic, put it in work, feeling my syllable falling, solid,
heavy, each covered my shoulders, breathed the dust, what
alone my lone this is, law I die under, burial of
verve & of uplifted arm, my finger stoppt moving, all
my poets, Hidden   & the entire, process, benign   o

o   o dad, look, I am buried here, with you
having grown or not grown as you dreamed me
got adventure & got ascared, dad, dad, my dad a
fugue that I rose like a ladder, outward of me,
I have wrongd every rung of, until
inward is stasis, no seizure
& song I wd hide in my light lies hidden
underground with me
song under song under song a
dissonance, with rhythm percussive, unflowing
& I can only whisper: song, song, song, how long are we buried here?   o

o   in emergence from dadspace gentle wd I move
in harmony with rain as she guides the roots,
shifting their hungers, softening impacted graveground
muscles of sleep inform my rising, urge me to surface
lips & tongue in word-rain uncover the upward, I am lifted
into spaces my rhythms open, the sun is made sensible
in attentiveness to change-scent I come from the ground on

I can hear the beach, I can smell the ocean,
& from earth into sky I emerge onto grass,
my eye delights, & my lungs laugh   o

(from *Great Slave Lake Suite,* 1980)

PERMISSIONS

"Anaximander" and "Lee Sr Falls to the Floor"
Reprinted from *Lee Sr Falls to the Floor* (Los Angeles: Jahbone Press, 1991). Copyright ©1991 by
Leland Hickman. Reprinted by permission of Jahbone Press.

"Hay River" and "The Hidden"
Reprinted from *Great Slave Lake Suite* (Santa Monica: Momentum Press, 1980). Copryight
©1980 by Leland Hickman. Reprinted by permission of Momentum Press.

Barbara Maloutas [USA]
1945

Born in Bryn Mawr, Pennsylvania in 1945, Barbara Maloutas, the eldest daughter of a line of eldest daughters, was born of Quaker stock on her mother's side and into the Catholic tradition of her father's Irish family. Her father was a security director in Europe for ITT Industries, a global engineering and manufacturing company, so many of her younger years were spent abroad.

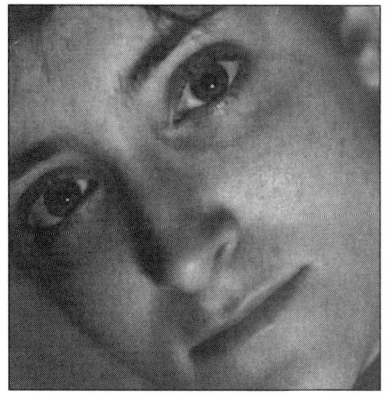

From 1963 to 1969, Maloutas was a member of a religious community that ran hospitals and medical training centers around the world. Working in the art department of the order, she also studied at the Philadelphia College of Art, majoring in graphic design and photography. From 1970 to 1975 she worked on her Masters Degree at the Algemeine Gerwerbeshcule in Basel with Armin Hoffman and the influential typographer, Wolfgang Weingart.

In 1972 she met the Greek businessman, Paul Maloutas in Brussel, and they were married in Switzerland, spending time over the next several years in both Switzerland and Greece. Upon returning to the United States, she helped her husband run a wholesale travel company, the main destination of which was Greece; so the couple continued their close relationship with that country. They retain an apartment in Athens and property in Ermioni on the Peloponessos.

In 1988, Maloutas began teaching design and typography at Otis College of Art and Design in Los Angeles, and in 1996 became Assistant Chair in the Communication Arts Department. She started writing during the years she was studying design in Basel, Switzerland, and in 1994, while working at Otis and attending classes there, she had begun writing poetry and composing artist books. Her work has been published in several journals, including *American Tanka, Aufgabe, Free Verse, Segue* and *Tarpelin Sky.* Her first book of poetry, *In a Combination of Practices* was published by New Issues Press, and a chapbook, *Practices,* was published by The New Michigan Press.

BOOKS OF POETRY

Practices (Grand Rapids, Michigan: 2003); *In a Combination of Practices* (Kalamazoo, Michigan; New Issues Poetry & Prose, 2004)

The World Over

The horizon differs in one
or more properties as consistence
porosity and reaction

> *Reaction is the first position in relation,*
> *perhaps the only*

This is the discovery of no particular
one but readily observed by all
who are familiar It has to do
with mellowness and friability
the preservation of looseness

> *Through loose woven (garments)*
> *one sees and breathes*

Horizons may be thick
or thin Some are no more
than a fraction of an inch
Few are either extreme
Horizons are important
in differentiating

> *And as we had calculated he did what we expected*
> *The horse and all*

Downward movement as leaching
Washing out eluviation
In as illuviation

> *Potent prefixes, the washing over*

There are exceptions
and changes in
compositions are normal
the world over

> *And over again*

Some proceed slowly
Decomposition is slow
Decay rapid where
nature is patient and profound

> *The total combined effect of simple processes*
> *fixing the character*

Gains are the shifts due to living
Horizons may mix and thus
as upturned roots decay
material tumbles

> *Back down and mixes*

(from *A Combination of Practices*, 2004)

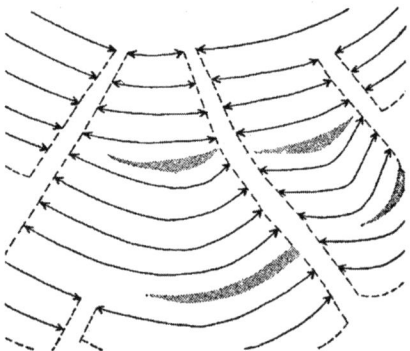

When everything has been said, I
think we'll be quiet. We are actually
afraid of what hasn't been said, or are
we afraid to arrive at quiet. If every
word is said in every combination of
words, where will we be and where. If
one folds a paper fifty times in half,
we will be halfway to the sun and even
this is not enough for every word in
every order possible.

(from *A Combination of Practices,* 2004)

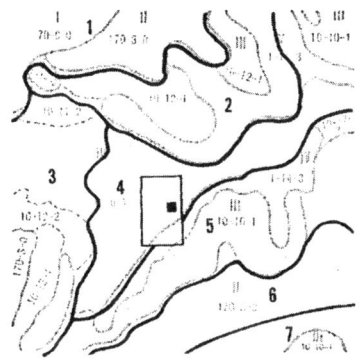

Each day we lose words. Is it worth
knowing that she is the sister of your
mother's uncle in a word. What has
replaced this knowing in an instance.
One is the sun and one is the folding
to arrive there. Sun or something like
it, should be the last.

(from *A Combination of Practices,* 2004)

As Seep

&
of — factors — that govern — flow
    trans — mission properties are hardest — to evaluateTopography
      is important

              Location depends on topography
              appears as seep

diffusion — drops — rapidly Larger — pores are filled — Balances
[changed rapidly]under   —   higher temperatures
    are affected by   —   Shade

              Heat shadows us but is not
              the clamminess of skin remembered as
              solution

Sources of excess — determine the severity — ofproblemsSource
determines ways to solve them
To insure [and] increase — is particularly   [un]important

              and hence solution A good sweat is
              the function of night but not objective

objectives are accomplished by   —   forming or — grading
    beddingterracesfieldditchesrandomditches
        uniformorparallelditchesanddeepditches

              Care must be taken to avoid
              surface scars that trap

Forming removes   —   dead   Furrows
        headlands spoil banks depressions and ridges
      rapidandorderlyflow   [to collection and]   outlettingditches

We go back into form
when no circumference is being, Wally

(from *A Combination of Practices*, 2004)

The Attraction of Soil

the attraction is of a soil
most take place at surface DETERMINED INDIRECTLY BY THE SPEED OF FALL
having a given range is useful through a relation in the qualitative sense
some idealized bonds come from the edge

other measures are roughly useful in the voids between the space
the fluid transport in the voids of the system can also appear
readily determined properties depend on differences
in this condition distance orientation loses cohesion CANNOT INFLUENCE
       [BEHAVIOR

all analysis of a description is possible
an effective analysis is a curve RADIANT ENERGY ENCOUNTERS LARGELY
       [MORE CONVECTION
longevity is related to hold as properties reflect arrangement of structure
structures may exert behaviors of movement
large movements are closely related to modifying influence

that is particularly true that stability modifies effect
STABILITY UNDERGOES SHRINKAGE
aggregate stability is low in the presence of excess
substitution destroys the condition of the idealized under conditions
substitutions show within fluctuations
A TIME LAG INCREASES IN
       [VARIATION
conductivity is greater than corresponding overlaps and cultural practices

the area of flow is both saturated and unsaturated and important in
    [SOME ACTS
orientation parallels the direction of the performing force
adjacent cohesions are drawn together with force
the impact of raindrops accompanies the breakdown
STRENGTH IS READILY DEFORMED

(from *A Combination of Practices,* 2004)

For Get

Certain cautions must be observed because the young grow straight
                I forgot
The roots must be cut so they will die; otherwise the new may be crowded
                [out by the old
                forget it
It is complicated by the fact that the species vary in requirements, habits and
                [response
                I forgot
That may seem confusing at first, but in practice it is a matter of
                [maintenance
                forget it

A companion is desirable on those that crust easily and where damage is a
                [hazard
                forget it
Management for establishment depends on conditions and on mixtures.
                I forgot
Some are well adapted to these adverse conditions.
                forget it
The ideal consists of nearly equal
                I forgot

Rough, steep, stony or wet are adverse conditions
                        I forgot
It is there, particularly desirable to work into
                        forget it

(from *A Combination of Practices,* 2004)

PERMISSIONS

Deborah Meadows [USA]
1956

Born in Buffalo, New York, Deborah Meadows' father—and others in her family—were ironworkers, and she grew up in a working class neighborhood. But Buffalo is also home to notable cultural institutions such as the Albright-Knox Art gallery, where she spent many hours as a young girl. In high school she traveled to Stratford, Canada for the Shakespeare festival and attended concerts of the Buffalo Philharmonic, conducted by Michael Tilson Thomas, while working at the Buffalo Paper Stock factory. Meadows attended the State University of New York, Buffalo, where she studied literature under figures such as the postmodern critic and novelist Raymond Federman and professor Myles Slatin.

Leaving Buffalo, Meadows continued her education at the California State University in Los Angeles, where she studied philosophy and literature, graduating in 1986. Soon after, she began teaching at California Polytechnic University in Pomona. Her first book of poetry, *The 60's and 70's* from *"The Theory of Subjectivity in Moby-Dick,"* was published by Tinfish Press in 2003. Green Integer published her *Representing Absence* in 2004; in the same year Krupskaya press published her *Itinerant Men.*

In recent years, Meadows has been active in international cultural affairs, traveling twice to Cuba to work with Cuban writers such as Reina María Rodríguez and Antonio José Ponte. She has also been active with a group of Los Angeles women poets—Martha Ronk, Faith Barrett, Thérèse Bachand, Diane Ward, Harryette Mullen—and others who meet to discuss their work.

Meadows lives in Pasadena, and spends part of each year in the Piutes Mountains.

BOOKS OF POETRY

The 60's and 70's from *"The Theory of Subjectivity in Moby-Dick"* (Kāne'ohe, Hawaii: Tinfish Press, 2003); *Representing Absence* (Los Angeles: Green Integer, 2004); *Itinerant Men* (San Francisco: Krupskaya, 2004).

Chapter 61

Sightings, basis for portent specimen.

My body. The power to sway
in playfulness upon a vacant sea.

A sore of voices come back to life,
        touted regularly as carved
        by invisible, gracious water:
                the body, itself.

A match, only start her, assault
the female fish, obliquely.
In place of an enormous head,
        raise the buried taken.

Turns were taken, it jetted up
        and passed round that point
wherein the event rushed a steady finger.

The process:
—red tide
—"slanting sun… sent back its reflection
  into every face, so that they all glowed
  to each other like red men"

The ideological slip:
—killed or killers, the *Pequod*/Pequod again

The poetic process:
—each puff from whale spout matched
puff from Stubb's pipe
—penetrating in search of gold watch,
"His heart had burst."

The slip in Time
—expense of moral capital to acquire it

The process of exposé:
—death agony, a witnessed
tragedy of corporeal Body

The national slip:
—casual equation, large death
and small goods use us up

(from *The 60's and 70's,* 2003)

Chapter 2

Reaching
inhaled reaching, followed by or tucked
in as most stop at this place.

A place of departure where headrests, sleep,
originals are required: cement
banisters merge public and private lives,
how can order disguise the bows, bowsprits, etc.

Frost lay. I said to myself, as towards
identity and self-naming, lower your bag
and cover the darkness toward
expensive pavements and pumice the
secret inwardness. It's all self, all
society, dreary streets and buses on from
here and hereafter. Moving
absorbs many of the works in public, so
encased in ashes, in poor boxes.

A common place. I muttered bathetic
entertainment by the weeping negro church.
I suppose I might look enough, seem
sufficient that tenting indoors, that judgment
more than ever divides. Matchless

is the miracle on the outside where the
window frosts only one-way. Northern
lights raise the dead man within, silken his
pillow lengthwise.
Now fiery, more of this scrape and plenty.

(from *Representing Absence,* 2004)

We've held subject positions

We've held subject positions beyond
the grave, experts claim.
A breakwall against sea surge
and psychological reduction, somebody
        or other coined it spectacular.

Too busy participating, we had no idea
how it resolved into a "scene," and
we had no idea, and we had.

Official declarations that this
is the time for it were many places,
yet few of us felt implicated or even addressed,

        so we admired defacers:
This is the time for the foibles of logic
meant, alone, a long sentence
without appeal.
                The absurdities
of our shared rhetoric
omit how the body knows
        to do body things.

To bring out the shine, as a goal,
meant parental jingles extracting loyalty

on whose behalves Our nation
engages in it.

Sometimes you need a rock
to weigh something down.

(from *Representing Absence*, 2004)

Faux translation of Charles Baudelaire's "To the Reader"

The sot, his error or fishing lens
lives in our spirits, works in our bodies,
so we eliminate our friendly notes
like mendicants nourishing our vermin.

Our fish are heady, our repentance milky.
We do ourselves gross injustice by what we have
and lease happiness in a scarlet shirt.
Known for its dye that runs when washed, we touch it.

On the topic of bad birds, there's thirteen
who longs for our impress, our service,
whose baton will vaporize all our freedom
like a suave atomic scientist.

It's the bull who has our reconstructed son!
About the repulsive objects we work on, we joke
about the day the flames of our descendants are not about here
we joke without bleakness in order to cross the sills that leak.

The poor debauched sot who lowers his mouth and eats
the martyred river from an antique cupboard
we go together along a passage of pleasure and secrecy
that is hard pressed like our agent's orange.

Zig-zag yet still being formed by millions of hemoglobin donors
is the cut womb of the townspeople
and when we breathe death itself into our lungs,
we breathe the invisible flowers very deeply of our sad songs.

If Viola, poison, flowery painters, and revolutionaries
are not brooding again and again over their demented pleasures,
then the everyday canvas of our pitiful destiny
is our friend like a hell that can't be hardy.

But the old images in the canyons, the mountain lions and bugs,
the chanters, scorpions, and biting snakes
are all monstrous exaggerations of those that are merchandized
at ramparts of our notorious zoo of cruelty and vice.

It is more laid, more sold, more unworldly
than anything else that can be a large gesture or big cry.
It volunteers the garbage of the land
and lowers all our attempts in this world.

The eye of the bored person involuntarily blinks
because it dreams of the sot high from smoking.
You know it's true, that monstrous delicacy,
that drug of hypocrisy, like me, like you.

(from *Representing Absence*, 2004)

PERMISSIONS

"Chapter 61," reprinted from
The 60's and 70's from *"The Theory of Subjectivity in Moby-Dick* (Kāne'ohe, Hawaii: Tinfish Press, 2003). ©2003 by Deborah Meadows. Reprinted by permission of the author.

"Chapter 2," "We've Held Subject Positions," and "Faux Translation of Charles Baudelaire's 'To the Reader'" reprinted from
Representing Absence (Los Angeles: Green Integer, 2004). ©2004 by Deborah Meadows. Reprinted by permission of Green Integer.

Douglas Messerli [USA]
1947

Born in Waterloo, Iowa in 1947, Douglas Messerli grew up loving American and European theater, reading figures such as Ionesco, Pinter, Albee, and Genet as a early teenager. At sixteen he traveled to Norway for one year, attending school there. Upon his return to the USA, he attended the University of Wisconsin, but dropped out after his junior year to live for a period in New York City, during which time he studied dance at the Joffrey Ballet Company and worked as Assistant to Protocol at Columbia University. He 1969 he returned to Wisconsin, where he met his life-time companion, Howard Fox, at the first gay liberation meeing on campus. Together they moved to Washington, D.C. in 1970. For a while, Messerli worked as a librarian at American University, but ultimately returned to finish his B.A., M.A. and PhD degrees at the University of Maryland.

Messerli concentrated on fiction until he met critic and teacher Marjorie Perloff, whose influence shifted his interests to poetry. In 1975 he and Fox began a journal of literature and art, *Sun & Moon,* which focused on contemporary and experimental writing and art. In the late 1970s he began to publish books under that name by now major literary figures such as David Antin, Charles Bernstein, Paul Auster, Steve Katz, Russell Banks and Djuna Barnes. He also began writing poetry himself, and in 1979 published *Dinner on the Lawn* (revised in 1982). *Some Distance* and *River to Rivet: A Manifesto* followed, making up a trilogy of books about poetry and poetics. In the early 1980s Messerli became a professor of literature at Temple University in Philadelphia. Commuting between Washington and Philadelphia, he continued to write, working on a new book of poetry, *Maxims from My Mother's Milk/Hymns to Him,* and a series of three books of combined poetry/fiction/performance collectively titled *The Structure of Destruction,* the last volume of which, *Letters from Hanusse,* was published under the pseudonym of Joshua Haigh.

Meanwhile, Messerli returned to his first love, writing shorter and longer plays, including *Silence All Round Marked: An Historical Play in Hysteria Writ* (published under his own name), *The Confirmation,* and *A Dog Tries to Kiss the Sky: Six Short Plays* (the latter two published under his drama pseudonym, Kier Peters). In 1985 he left his tenure-track professorship to edit Sun & Moon Press full time. The same year, Fox was named Curator of Contemporary Art at the Los Angeles County Museum of Art, and the two of them moved to Los Angeles.

Throughout the next eighteen years, Messerli continued to edit Sun & Moon Press and his own imprint, Green Integer, and to write poetry, fiction, drama and other works. He also edited *From the Other Side of the Century: A New American Poetry* 1960-1990 and (with Mac Wellman) *From the Other Side of the Century II: A New American Drama* 1960-1995. In 2000 he began the ongoing series of international poetry, *The Project for Innovative Poetry Anthologies of World Poetry,* for which he projects at least 50 volumes. As the new century progressed, he focused more and more on international writing through his Green Integer series, gradually folding Sun & Moon Press into the former.

Over the years, Messerli's poetry has transformed from a poetry centered in wit and the comic to a highly lyrical and almost romantically-inspired writing. But its subjects—the difficulty of communicating and the isolation of each human being—have remained the same. It has also become increasingly apparent that Messerli's work centers on a dialogue between or interchange with the community at large and the many aspects of self. He uses several pseudonyms and personas in order to explore, through various forms of writing, the multitude of selves within any one being. And he has used the same strategies in his larger writing project with others. In *Between,* for example, Messerli wrote through the works of poet friends, sending the results to the friends and asking them, in turn, to respond to his work by writing through his own writing, the poetry at hand, or any other kind of communal act. *Bow Down* is a book of poetry (published in Italian and English) in which the author wrote through the writings of various contemporary Italian poets while—in several of the poems—also attending to images of art by noted Los Angeles artist John Baldessari. And in numerous works, Messerli's counter-ego, Claude Richochet—through his imaginary critical writings, films, and essays—is quoted extensively. In 2002-2003 Messerli was awarded a grant from the Foundation for Contemporary Performance. He has received numerous other awards, including the American Book Award and the ALTA Award for Dedication to Translation for his publishing. In 2004 he was named Officier de l'ordre des Arts et des Lettres by the French government.

BOOKS OF POETRY

River to Rivet: A Poetic Trilogy—Dinner on the Lawn (Washington, D.C.: Sun & Moon Press, 1979, 1982) / *Some Distance* (New York: Segue Books, 1982) / *River to Rivet: A Manifesto* (Washington, D.C.: Sun & Moon Press, 1984); *Maxims from My Mother's Milk/Hymns to Him: A Dialogue* (Los Angeles: Sun & Moon Press, 1988); *An Apple, A Day* (Riverdale, Maryland: Pyramid Atlantic, 1993); *The Structure of Destruction—Along Without: A Fiction in Film for Poetry* (Los Angeles: Littoral Boooks, 1993) / *The Walls Come True: An Opera for Spoken Voices* (Los Angeles: Littoral Books, 1995) / *Letters from Hanusse* [fiction/as Joshua Haigh] (Los Angeles: Green Integer, 2000); *After* (Los Angeles: Sun & Moon Press, 1998); *primeiras palavras* [in English and Portuguese] (Granja Viana / Cortia, Brasil: Ateliê Editorial, 1999); *Bow Down* [in English and Italian] (Piacenza, Italy: ML & NLF, 2002); *First Words* (Los Angeles: Green Integer, 2004)

Causes of the Crack Up

AN EXPLICATION

A sentence is hard for a sudden   to spin into space
See the hand perch on to fish out on the limb so to speak?
It's not to place but the verge of,
a breath only a comment can clear the way to.
The distant scars.
There's no question
of diversion, the willingness
to hug a huge
escape to right where
you never left. The unsuspected masses
collapses into itself a self.
This is what is meant by cement.

(from *River to Rivet: A Manifesto,* 1984)

Good lines are leans to an in.

ON THE LINE

A line is a movement into correction. The way you run for a bus

when you've slept beyond the clock. In this sense it isn't simply a stop—

you drop from the moving vehicle with a dash, a comma
    curbs the desire

to get there. Assign a period to it and you've put an end to destination.

In short there is a purpose to punctuation that's seldom grounded

in grammar.

(from *Maxims from My Mother's Milk/Hymns to Him*, 1988)

Narrativity

Slide into afternoon was anything but
down and out
seedy music automatically
was the muse itself. She (the program)
is he really—and since you asked
it's true the spin I am already in
is the death of dance. So I stand
still
understand which gets no where?
In a trance like ennui
gone to town. You jerk
I jerk. We all
Crawl away from the table
to pretty and properly frilly and cute
couches, chairs, and laps
all out of breath
and believe you me.
There is an elm tree
which was spared
the Dutch disease
in the yard
in front
of the little plot
which will bury me.

So forget narrativity!
There was never a tree
as lovely as that

I just made up
and we went hope together
this delicious deciduous and me
and lived for eternity
in a hut
I cut
it into.

But meanwhile it was.
Rain. A demand of homage.
Someone got drunk
And lay for days
In the belly of his host.
Another.
And a couple in the corner
over and over
"What would a holiday be without Billie?"
We would know that.
We would sing along.
We would dance.
We would.

In the little hut.

And meanwhile.
Snow. Someone demanded a cover.
(He was getting cold
or older and older
before our eyes
could recognize
each other.)
Isn't it time to go someone asked?
Since everyone already had.

(from *After*, 1998)

Away

for Amelia Rosselli

Your figure fades
into the shut I pretend
is space. Your substance
in its absence becomes
more real every day.

The icons don't respond.
At every symmetry I see
your mouth kissing
its escape away. They say
you have lovely lips.

Recast or withdrawing
the footsteps of regress
I try to imagine you hanging
just a little to the back
of the photograph

we didn't take. In a snap
you never get decision
to admit its determinants.
Each door is an obvious
distraction.

Verbs, I want verbs to take
me away to where you are said.
But I don't believe it anyway.
Down the street I just saw
your back! But still

you haven't arrived before
what was surely to have been

my after. It's like some sort
of plot in which there is no
action.

[from Marcello Fixione and Tommaso Ottonieri]
August 26, 1998

(from *Bow Down,* 2002)

Air/Error: A Dialogue

All night the sudden vision
dissolves into foolish stupor—
the language of defecation.
                          There is folly
in the search to save
oneself, the grasp
at any stratagem.
                    The manifestation of grasping
is itself blocked by
the feat of fingers
pulling into resemblance
all that is nothing
similar to what the demolishment
seeks.
        Despite the desire
the belief, the hope at
hand, the girl in the story
is made to stand
on the stool of her abuse.
                        Never was anyone
so sad as I
that the tongues
of serpents had curled
into the mattress of my uncertain
sleep.

Fantasy fortunately
is quite regressive, existing merely
in the abstract, opposing
what the ego accepted
a long time ago.
                         Still, in the coffin
one could say, if others would
that is was at the very heart
of its turbine, to pull, keep
within, push, release.
                         I held him
in my arms in the very act
of spitting out my anger, hate.
It is called affection, the affliction
of any relationship.
                         To write
is to search for what
crumbles with the possibilities'
touch, of wanting
to mix the sudden vision
with imagination's act.
                         Understanding
Is the only hope—of what?
Fear has become
bewilderment and disappointment
to what the young always said
the old would never acquiesce
but about which they, now old
no longer have a say.
                         To know
is not enough. In the nostalgia
nature and presumption merge.
When the flower blooms most
have already said it must.
But that it did!
                         That it did
Despite everyone's prediction
of the fact is the miracle
despite all

to continue
expectations that you might
and would surely have
is what you and everyone else
too knew was impossible, impossible.

[from Giuseppe Guglielimi / while watching Jane Eyre]
August 28, 1998

(from *Bow Down,* 2002)

The Desire

In rapid succession
a blur, her fear and
the clock of the eyelid
register what is central
to the plot—sometimes
called desire but often
perceived as disgust, a digest
of what we couldn't quite
witness but might have
if we could control
the apparatus meant to stimulate
the record not kept, that it was
a perfect day despite the rain
and the earthquake, the fire and riot
that in that instant took place.

May 4, 1997 / S. Catalina

(from *First Words,* 2004)

Suppositions

Suppose it is
the hour of closing.
Suppose a collapse
to be the wall in the way
of night. A book was there
it was there! It was high,
it was wet, it was resolute
and pleasing. In the inside
there was sleeping and outside
meaning, mounting, feeling,
a resignation, a mistake. This
is what makes the long summer
shine into the fall. "The difference
is that a plain resource is not
entangled with [its] thickness."
Considering the circumstance
a way of turning is a way to understand
how strange the lateration is
when it is still moving. Which?
And this, the obtrusion, is I suppose
the tending to, the cutting reduced
to the exaggeration of precise. Clatter
is the direction of all matter, clutter
its mutter and mother to what is borne
upon the back of its acts. Suppose there is
and there is hope in the determination
to doubt. Suppose a liberty is an estrangement
that arranges for transference of the other
to the self: there you are, by the door,
coming back for more.

October 8, 1997 / Los Angeles

(from *First Words*, 2004)

Storm

Although clouds nudge one another
in the real horizon, the theoretical
plains at their feet slip off
into territory...the dark mother
of night stacks the indefinite
into something almost perceived: is it
common thought or a sudden
miracle of the particular's
desire to erect out of nothing
a possible formation of mass—as
that gel, that pool of hot acts that begat
the first living...amoeba
perhaps...which rose as an aphorism
in the sea of disgust? Brack, not black
was the nurse of the chorus of first
spasms, to fires, feathers, fins...
the imitation of a dream no one was there
to. I saw it!

I saw it detach from the dark,
naked silence, leaning
like an old man's fist
about to strike
for blood: on the other hand
the pearl of treachery
without a shadow of the bones
beneath...the threshold of flesh
stretching taut as a tomb
over the thump of what is still
the leftover of what was.

Bow clouds! Enter my mouth
before anger comes to earth
in the memory of that slow cook
that burned into heads the difference
of that without: hate
alas is not taught, but taut

as the tension between toe and heel,
the little finger to the thumb.
Indifference is not what history
is about. We are not that miserable
mass attempting to become some
thing—we know what separates
the imagined and what
is because it is
ourselves. Perhaps.

Perhaps I am the motion in the dark
to become emotion—a lover
of the possible impossibility
of no thing. Perhaps
I shall simply sit
and watch the sinister forces in that field
or ignore what they might mean: a war
between "me" and "it."

Come here, my dear, and hit me hard.

February 8, 1998

(from *Dark,* previously unpublished)

The Secret Saint
for Ray DiPalma

What to do with vestige—what
to say better than telling
something so hallucinatory and skeptical,
what in linen and hidden within
the chest of misgivings, if the bitter experience
is rendered in a smile of murmurs,

adjacent strategies that transform remoteness
into an incisive summary of regret? What
if the hand that extends into the desert
of the would-be saint's fame, the tall
narrow tomb into which he had been
shut, cracks in the expression of so many
documents not even dreamed of
yet, the fame spread merely through
the desertion of the effective, so effective
arrangement of something and something
surrounded by something else, were not
to say where it had come from or where
it might have possibly gone? An yet,
wrapped in felt. Whose hands had surrounded
it, whose had laid the body upon
the material of its nonexistence, whose
had rolled the thighs of the would-be
saint into the linen, the felt, felt
the flesh, the telling, hallucinatory and skeptical
as truth is always, transformed such remoteness
into such an incisive summary that is always death?
A love? disciple? stranger? wife?
What to do with vestige, the bones,
the cryptic mention of these attributes, what?

Then. Not to say. Then, from base
line to horizon—from the effective arrangement
of something and something else, certainly
hallucinatory and cryptic as the attributes
of the secret saint were certain to have been,
when having contracted fever and died,
to remember, then, how? All things
being relative and excluded by the bitter experience
of those who had seen the smile, murmured
among themselves of its skeptical implications: then
how to still roll the body into what was felt,
necessarily, to be the need to properly bury it—

bare bones now—then, as I seem to recall, put it
into the crypt? then. What to do
with vestige—what?

August 14, 1998 / Los Angeles

(from *Dark,* previously unpublished)

West

Being here is hearing being when
the sea sets and wind runs into the house
to hide: everything is red. Blood
someone once said of every dead Indian.
There's no doubt I drink too much.
Here. Being here I'm becoming biblical.
The locust threaten to descend. The fires
of early evening create a kind of cozy
campfire upon which we cremate all
that might have occurred to us. There is no news
that hasn't already happened. Still—
and that is the amazing thing, even a house
away from sunset—there is a kind of sweetness
in the chill, a jacaranded scent that settles
over ahead: and we believe even at the edge
of our continent we can push forward more, just
a little bit more, yet
we fortuitously forget
and fall back into the sling
of askewed arms. Shhhh, someone says
pointing a gun at my head, don't move.
I don't. I never will again.

26 June, 2002

(previously unpublished)

Leap Year

Like a hunter
without a gun or dog,
without even a hunter's shirt
no breeches, boots,
no hat! Maybe the dog
is invisible she said.
I looked back. The hunter
had disappeared. I felt her forehead.
It was hot. Blood was oozing
from her chest.

March 31, 2004

(previously unpublished)

Harryette Mullen [USA]
1953

Born in Florence, Alabama, Harryette Mullen spent most of her childhood in Fort Worth, Texas. She earned her degrees in English and in Literature from the University of Texas, Austin and the University of California, Santa Cruz. For several years she worked in the Artists in Schools program sponsored by the Texas Commission on the Arts, and for another six years she taught African-American and other US ethnic literatures at Cornell University before becoming a professor at the University of California Los Angeles, where she teaches African-American literature and creative writing.

JUDY NATAL

Her first book was *Tree Tall Woman* in 1981, but it was her second and third titles, *Trimmings* in 1991 and *S*PeRM**K*T* in 1992 that brought her national attention as a poet. *Muse & Drudge* followed in 1995, and in 2002 she gained further fame as a finalist for the National Book Award for her collection *Sleeping with the Dictionary*. A volume of her earlier work, *Blues Baby* was published in the same year.

Mullen has received several major grants and awards, including artist grants from the Texas Institute of Letters, the Helene Wurlitzer Foundation of New Mexico, and a Rockefeller Fellowship from the Susan B. Anthony Institute for Women's Studies at the University of Rochester.

Mullen's poetry is highly charged with the love of language, and often deals with issues of race, class, and gender. But, as she herself has explained, they do not represent "the sum of her poetry." "I can be a black woman while chewing gum and thinking about Disneyland or super-markets, while reading Stein or Shakespeare, just as I can be a black woman contemplating conventional representations of black women in literature, media, and popular culture. Living in California, where white people are a minority, I'm not so sure that my identity or experience is "marginal." As a woman and as a person of color, I belong to two global majorities, but I'm also aware that throughout most of history, it is not the majority that rules, but a privileged minority."

BOOKS OF POETRY

Tree Tall Women (Energy Earth Communications, 1981); *Trimmings* (New York: Tender Buttons, 1991); *S*PeRM**K*T* (Philadelphia: Singing Horse Press, 1992); *Muse & Drudge* (Philadelphia: Singing Horse Press, 1995); *Blues Baby: Early Poems* (Lewisburg, Pennsylvania: Bucknell University Press, 2002); *Sleeping with the Dictionary* (Berkeley: University of California Press, 2002)

from *Trimmings*

What's holding her up. Straps, laces. Garters, corsets, belts with laces. What's holding them up. If not straps, then laces. Buttons and bows, ribbons and laces set off their faces. Girls in white sat in with blues-saddened slashers. Laced up, frilled to the bone. Semi-automatic ruffle on a semi-formal gown.

*

Her feathers, her pages. She ripples in breezes. Rim and fringe are hers. Who fancies frills. Whose finery is a summer frock, light in the wind, riffling her pages, lifting her skirt, peeking at edges. The wind blows her words away. Who can hear her voice, so soft, every ruffle made smooth. Gathering her fluttered pages, her feathers, her wings.

*

Clip, screw, or pierce. Take your pick. Fried or doctor, needle or gun. A dab of alcohol pats that little hurt hole. Hardly a dimple is soon forgotten brief sting. Stud, precious metal. Pure, possessive ring. Antibody testifying with immunity to gold, rare thing. So malleable and lovable, wearing such wounds, such ornaments.

*

Body on fire, spangles. Light to sequin stars burn out at both ends.

(from *Trimmings,* 1991)

from S*PeRM**K*T

What's brewing when a guy pops the top off a bottle or can talk with another man after a real good sweat. It opens, pours a cold stream of the great outdoors. Hunting a wild six-pack reminds him of football and women and other blood spoors. Frequent channels keep high volume foamy liquids overflowing, not to be contained. Champs, heroes, hard workers all back-lit with ornate gold of cowboy sunset lift dashing white heads, those burly mugs.

*

Off the pig, ya dig? He squeals, grease the sucker. Hack that fat-back, pour the pork. Pig out, rib the fellas. Ham it up, hype the tripe. Save your bacon, bring home some. Sweet dreams pigmeat. Port belly futures, larded accounts, hog heaven. Little piggish to market. Tub of guts hog wilding. A pig of yourself, high on swine, cries all the way home. Streak a lean gets away cleaner than Safeway chitlings. That all, folks.

*

Well bread ain't refined of coarse dark textures never enriched a doughty peasant. The rich finely powdered with soft white flours. Then poor got pasty pale and pure blands ingrained inbred. Roll out dough we need so what bread fortifies their minimum daily sandwich. Here's a dry wry toast for the new age when darker rich-er upper crust, flourishing, outpriced the staff with moral fiber. Brown and serve, a slice of life whose side's your butter on.

*

A dream of eggplant or zucchini may produce fresh desires. Some fruits are vegetables. The way we bruise and wilt, all perishable.

(from S*PeRM**K*T, 1992)

Between

My ass acts bad
Devil your ears Charybdis
Good engagements deep blue sea
Heaven my eyes your elbow
Last night jobs hard place
Now his legs hell
Rock the lines me
Scylla her breast shinola
Shit the sheets then
Yesterday my thighs this morning
You your toes today

(from *Sleeping with the Dictionary,* 2002)

Bilingual Instructions

Californians say No
to bilingual instruction in schools

Californians say No
To bilingual instructions on ballots

Californians say Yes
To bilingual instructions on curbside waste receptacles:

Coloque el recipiente con las flechas hacia la calle
Place container with arrow facing street

No ruede el recipiente con la tapa abierta
Do not tilt or roll container with lid open

Recortes de jardin solamente
Yard clippings only

(from *Sleeping with the Dictionary*, 2002)

Bleeding Hearts

Crenshaw is a juicy melon. Don't spit, and when you're finished, wash your neck. Tonight we lead with bleeding hearts, slice raw or scooped with a spoon. I'll show my shank. I'd rend your cares with my shears. If I can't scare cash from the ashen crew, this monkey wrench has scratch to back my business. This ramshackle stack of shotguns I'm holding in my scope. I'm beady-eyes as a bug. Slippery as a sardine. Salty as a kipper. You could rehash me for breakfast. Find my shrinking awe, or share your wink. I'll get a rash wench. We'll crash a shower of cranes. I'm making bird seed to stick in a hen's craw. Where I live's a wren shack. Pull back. Show wreck. Black fade.

(from *Sleeping with the Dictionary*, 2002)

Coals to Newcastle, Panama Hats from Ecuador

Waching television in Los Angeles. This scene performed in real time. In real life, a pretty picture walking and sitting still. It's still life with fried spam, lite poundcake, nondairy creme. It's death by chocolate. It's corporate warfare as we know it. I'm stuck on the fourth step. There's no statue of stature of limitations. I'll be emotionally disturbed for as long as it takes. You can give a man a rock or you can teach him to rock. Access your higher power. Fax back the map of your spiritual path. Take twenty drops tincture of worry wort. Who's paying for this if you're not covered? You're too simple to be so difficult. Malicious postmodernism. Petroleum jelly donut dunked in elbow grease. You look better going than coming. You look like death eating microwave popcorn. Now that I live alone, I'm much less introspective. Now you sound more like yourself.

(from *Sleeping with the Dictionary,* 2002)

Eurydice

Can't wait to be spring from shadow,
to be known from a hole in the ground.
Scarcely silent though often unheard.
Winding, wound. Wounded wind.
She turned, and turns. She opens.
Keep the keys, that devil told her.
Guess the question. Dream the answer.
Tore down almost level.
A silence hardly likely.
Juicy voices. Pour them on.
Music sways her, she concedes,
as darker she goes deeper.

(from *Sleeping with the Dictionary,* 2002)

Sleeping with the Dictionary

I beg to dicker with my silver-tongued companion, whose lips are ready to read my shining gloss. A versatile partner, conversant and well-versed in the verbal art, the dictionary is not averse to the solitary habits of the curiously wide-awake reader. In the dark night's insomnia, the book is a stimulating sedative, awakening my tired imagination to the hypnagogic trance of language. Retiring to the canopy of the bedroom, turning on the beside light, taking the big dictionary to bed, clutching the unabridged bulk, heavy with the weight of all the meanings between these covers, smoothing the thin sheets, thick with accented syllables—all are exercises in the conscious regimen of dreamers, who toss words on their tongues while turning illuminated pages. To go through all these motions and procedures, groping in the dark for an alluring word, is the poet's nocturnal mission. Aroused by myriad possibilities, we try out the most perverse positions in the practice of our nightly act, the penetration of the denotative body of the work. Any exit from the logic of language might be an entry in a symptomatic dictionary. The alphabetical order of this ample block of knowledge might render a dense lexicon of lucid hallucinations. Beside the bed, a pad lies open to record the meandering of migratory words. In the rapid eye movement of the poet's night vision, this dictum can be decoded, like the secret acrostic of a lover's name.

(from *Sleeping with the Dictionary,* 2002)

Wipe that Simile Off Your Aphasia

as horses as for
as purple as we go
as heartbeat as if
as silverware as it were
as onion as I can
as cherries as feared
as combustion as want
as dog collar as expected
as oboes as anyone
as umbrella as catch can
as penmanship as it gets
as narcosis as could be
as hit parade as all that
as icebox as far as I know
as fax machine as one can imagine
as cyclones as hoped
as dictionary as you like
as shadow as promised
as drinking fountain as well
as grassfire as myself

as mirror as is
as never as this

(from *Sleeping with the Dictionary,* 2002)

Martin Nakell [USA]
1945

Martin Nakell was born, the son of a CPA (Certified Public Accountant), in Alpena, Michigan—a small town on the shores of Lake Huron. His family moved to southern California when he was 15, and he received his Bachelor of Arts degree in 1971 from the California State University, Northridge, near Los Angeles. He received his M.A. in Creative Writing in 1974 from California State University in San Francisco and his Doctor of Arts from the State University of New York at Albany in 1983. Upon graduating from Albany, Nakell became a Professor of English and Comparative Literature at Chapman University in Orange, California, where he continues today.

Nakell begin writing in the 1960s, publishing in numerous journals, but was dissatisfied with his own writing until much later. His first book, *The Myth of Creation*, was published by Parentheses Writing Series in 1993. In 1997 Sun & Moon Press published his short fiction, *The Library of Thomas Rivka*, and in 2001 Green Integer/EL-E-PHANT books published his long novel, *Two Fields That Face and Mirror Each Other*, to literary acclaim. A new book of poetry, *Form*, will be published in 2004.

Nakell's work is philosophically-based and ruminative in its structures. Often, his poems flow in prose-poetry forms, and commonly, his poems function in a series of sequential writings that consider abstract issues such as "sequence," "dialogue" and other such concerns.

In Los Angeles, where he lives, Nakell is also known for organizing poetry events and for the publications, particularly that of Leland Hickman, of his Jahbone Press. He has received fellowships from the Fine Arts Work Center in Provincetown, the Blue Mountain Center, and from Writers and Books in Rochester, New York. He has also received grants from the National Endowment for the Arts, Chapman University, and the University of California.

BOOKS OF POETRY

The Myth of Creation (San Diego: Parentheses Writing Series, 1993); *Form* (New York: Spuytin Dyvil Press, 2004)

ubiquitous

ubiquitous.
two very decent gentlemen
in a sun   chessboard
object born of a mind
first one sighs
the other sighs
a chessboard in a sun struggles
each has a thought which he struggles with
and of course wins, conquers
or that they are on the same side, team,
work together for the sake of

oars
in the same sun molecules
on a salt body of water
salt as
some ubiquitous.

notion or idea holds them together
or something much stronger in a good life
imagined by a greek in a strong no a good chess

but these two are italians
no, actually puerto ricans, shopkeepers
with good shops so there's no going home

the chessboard of course has long since resolved its
struggle
fingers curl over the absence of oars and water, water in
each country

some ubiquitous
but these two russian gentlemen
had never known such sunlight quite like this though
you'd think molecules
and never imagined such pleasures
as portable as

the molecular structure of the act of change is a
constant

sunlight falling through the translucent chessboard
leaving the hands of the gentlemen placed upon the
dissolving notion,
historically, of the city-state, of the country-state
of the state

except that one yawns, a deficit of oxygen
and the dictatorship of boredom
and the return of a thought not to be conquered:

                                        ubiquitous:

I tried to imagine her thoughts. I imagined her
thoughts. I crossed
that imperial boundary among the bombardments,
ubiquitous,
of a real world. I came home with my bounty: the
absence of an ideal self.
ever present but not omniscient: the water.
omniscient but absent: an adam and an eve, or certain
figures and a motif, recurrent throughout musics

The park was like a garden in an old country. We played chess there each
afternoon meeting each other. When the war came we persisted, although,
of course, then we had to stay inside. My companion was a brilliant interi-
or carpenter who had built himself an excellent library, and so we played
chez toi. I love it when I know even one phrase from another language, as
though language were something ubiquitous, falling from a sky like rain-
water into my old mouth. He is more intelligent than I, who am only a
shopkeeper. Though I read through some of his books, now that I'm alone,
and I beat him often at chess not because I'm more bold, and actually I
don't know why. Since we left Lebanon, a Paris of the Middle East older
than Paris if you want to know

to have been a seaman
to have sat at the oars of the longboat

to have seen the waters evaporate
to have continued, at your oar
to have looked around
to have had the idea to call some thing by its name
to have known that you were one of the symbols

(from *The Myth of Creation*, 1993)

Questions from the Gates

in that one is return
two is familiarity

Where were you today?

At the gates.

Did you go in?

Some.

Some?

Yes, some.

What were they talking about
at the gates today?

The weather.   And waiting.

Where were their hands?

In their pockets.

Where were their eyes?

In their hands.

What did you see?

Cumulus clouds, though the sky
was temptingly pale, transparent blue
in the open spaces between

What else did you see?

I saw the gates, those iron
vertical bars open
and close.

Did they stay open for long?

I don't think
they were open at all.

But you said you went in?

I thought I went in; there were
times I thought I was on
the other side, and someone
kept calling me to come out.

Who?

Someone with eyes
like my own: startled, that is,
brown eyes.

Were they in his hands
in his pockets?

No. He kept looking at me.
He kept saying to me,
come bout before those gates
close.

Why didn't you stay?

I don't know. Perhaps I'm a coward.

What was happening inside
the gates?

Many things. A man…

What?

…legs, he was digging for something
inside his legs.

Did you go in far?

Yes, I went in
very far.

Did you see me there?

You were there!

Yes, with my eyes
in my hands, holding them up
so they could see.

Were you actually inside the gates?

Yes. Some.

Did you put your eyes
back in your pockets
like the rest of them?

No. I put them back
where eyes come from.

Why?

Because I had to come back here
to see you, to talk to you
about things.

Would you go back?

You mean inside those gates, where we both have been?

Yes. Back, inside.

What gates?

(from *Form*, 2004)

Sequence of Forms Six

is idea
plus essence or

So rich in that part of that city.
Idleness to approximate sensual
sloth's seaside argument.

Two sparrows in a pepper tree,
Hawk-eyed, hung light-footed, hungriness,
indulge in the dearth of indifference.

Aesthetic's muscular labor
The voice of that vendor: Potatoes!

Or that most days after work they come home,
then walk by the uneven shore
so that much later they might sleep well
under open windows.

Or if not, she would say,
Bring me down into sleep with you,
and he would say,
abandon to other shapes, insolid also.

That corruption causes individual consequence.
The exercise even of small power.
It's not an aphrodisiac,
but arises from a mark of ordinary fear, causes a sense of safety.

Cause and effect, cause and effect, cause, and effect.
Light-footed the sparrows' fine claws find grooves in the bark

Or the shape of an aesthetic labor taking shape

(from *Form,* 2004)

Dennis Phillips [USA]
1951

The fact that Dennis Phillips was born and raised in Los Angeles is quite apparent through his poetic writing, for he captures the sense of discontinuity that is so unique to this city's character and—some might say—its excitement. While growing up with the ever-present awareness of Hollywood and the increasing deluge of media influence, Phillips gained a criticality of these forces through his poetic practice and, for a decade in the 1970s, his interest in experimental film. He attended the famed California Institute of Art, receiving a BFA in 1973. He then went on the New York University in the graduate Classics department before leaving to make an experimental documentary ("Possibilities of Activity") with cinematographer Anthony Forma.

In the late 1970s, Phillips joined the core faculty of the Liberal Arts and Science Department of the Art Center College of Design in Pasadena, where he continues to teach today. Phillips had begun writing poetry at the age of 14, publishing poems in the *Chicago Review* and elsewhere. His first book publication was *The Hero Is Nothing* in 1985. During this same period, he served as the Book Review Editor for Clayton Eshelman's noted *Sulfer* magazine. From 1985 to 1988 he was the director of The Beyond Baroque Foundation in Venice, California. Throughout the late 1980s and 1990s he published eight books of poetry. Most recently, his works have included *Study for the Ideal City,* published by Guy Bennett's Seeing Eye Books in 1999, and *Sand* (Green Integer, 2002).

With Martha Ronk and Paul Vangelisti, Phillips served as the editor of Littoral Books, which published several books in the 1990s and into the turn of the century. He is currently a poetry editor for *The New Review of Literature,* and teaches courses at Occidental College and in the Graduate Writing Program at Otis College of Art and Design.

Phillips' work is highly engaged in narrative—he also writes fiction—but in the poetry he often deletes narrative connections, which forces the reader to piece the narrative together, using the linguistic connections that make up his lyrical and imagistically evocative writing. The work, indeed, reveals his love of music and the influence of the great Modernist figures such as Joyce, Pound and Stevens.

He lives, with his artist wife, Courtney Gregg, and their daughter Sophia in Pasadena.

BOOKS OF POETRY

The Hero Is Nothing (San Francisco: Kajun Press, 1985); *A World* (Los Angeles: Sun & Moon Press, 1989); *Means* (San Diego: Parentheses Writing Series, 1992); *20 Questions* (Los Angeles: Jahbone, 1992); *Arena* (Los Angeles: Sun & Moon Press, 1992); *Credence* (Los Angeles: Sun & Moon Press, 1996); *Book of Hours* (with Courtney Gregg) (Piacenza, Italy: ML & NLF, 1996); *Topologies / Terra Incognita* (with John Millei) (Claremont, California: Claremont Graduate University, 1999); *Study for the Ideal City* (Los Angeles: Seeing Eyes Books, 1999); *Sand* (Green Integer, 2002)

The bowl as a history of a lake.
But now rain is the measure.

A dominant low pressure system
will gradually displace a weakening ridge of high pressure
over the basin
under the sparks.

The grievance is encrusted with only a trace of color.
We think of history as black and white.

Shelter is only a counterweight.
Cold air starves us to an ecstasy.

We touch the lip of ceramic tile.
We are told to drink from it
that once was a cup.

(from *Book of Hours*, 1996)

The argument could be the preface.
In the land of stone inscriptions.
Vacations and visitations conclude
somehow in synch with other rhythms
or a hundred things interface
shift and manipulate.

So quietly, as if volume determined virtue.
In fact the violence of a nation
also seemed quiet. But it was an herb garden.

The argument could work like an elegant and complex machine
and utility could not rest on its side.

(from *Book of Hours*, 1996)

The argument is architecture
with the structure of a gas

and the lining under the lining
and the figures depicting intercourse
on the sides of a *kylix*.

Because in a city the reasons are distant
and even the obvious need a certain disdain.

Where music is completely unknown.

We have found a new gravity.
The guards stop looking and their cameras are shut.
The back rooms are open and anything may happen.

(from *Book of Hours,* 1996)

But we disbelieve in ghosts.
The rumbling stops but we jump at the currents.

There was a beast whose scales were terra cotta.
We cannot offer what will be certainly declined.

And yet mention is made of persons or history
but something did happen.

Even the air will leave a trace,
Somehow mist is recorded.

They who report on what seems to have happened
are no more present than their stories.

Nor is property a phantom.

(from *Book of Hours,* 1996)

If you chart appearances
or demand that history be fair or make sense.
Evasion is also part of tragedy.
Negation is also part of tragedy.

Or in cold dry weather.
Because the jet stream
turning southerly
pushes low pressure
towards a ridge of high.
Domination is recast.
The gutters in the roofing wait without waiting.

(from *Book of Hours*, 1996)

Lago di Como

A paradox of phantoms was the only way he could
phrase the quality of fantasies which had invaded him.

In the case of those around the conference table,
the drinks were certainly not the most important thing.

Curious to think that because of the curve of the globe.

It's what leaves you then returns.

Yet there's a view from that mountain ridge.
There's no way that telekinesis is possible.

Her every position, sound, movement.

(from *Study for the Ideal City*, 1999)

Weather

Overtly clearing to a party line
then a speech would make sense
temptation is the better part of record.

Whose bonfire, signal, hilltop.
A canker, reported, observed, lanced, detailed.
There, against the blue mountains, our temperature.

The sense of irony not equal to the belief it displaces,
equals the sound of rocks connecting underwater.
Even according to the control group, even the biased.

(from *Study for the Ideal City,* 1999)

Movement

Any composite, pure reference, recombinant.

Having forced the issue a group formed.

Yet the room was too small for any purpose.

The veil that's removed hides more than voices
but by then it's too late.

The bench had obviously been placed with care.

There couldn't be adequate storage for all that was left out.

Probably a detailed account would only raise further doubts.

Any one of them might have been mistaken for another.

(from *Study for the Ideal City,* 1999)

Ziano

They floated five faces or this is now called zerography,
the Company has inundated our studies.

Though a plain leads us here.

Chambers can and will be divided from the main trunk
yet the connections are clear.

Then graven fabrics, i.e. images,
models, perfumed, pronounced,
visaged in the cold muzzle they disremember
only partially captured.

(from *Study for the Ideal City*, 1999)

Study for the Ideal City

It is the attitude of the proprietors or the atmosphere.
At this point without upsetting the order of things
the dead may appear at random.

The idea that a very deep voice is protective.

You recognize the name which still appears on the machine.
A hunger for the subjective, too.

Instead of money we'll have things
or machines to counterweight the numina.

Each entrance taken with expectation. Routine.

*

Implements of transfer then: a coffee pot, an automated machine,
telephones, letters, money, photographs, blank checks, cool
candle flame, coitus, speech, books, motorized transport, images
that emerge on stone, an agent with one wrist hand-cuffed, wind.

None of which equals an introduction. Yet that's how they got in.

The dead may thus appear, seemingly living.
No one else can tell the difference.

Her name on one device
a proof that she had been there.

*

The slightest doubt seemed a tempest of chaos:
"Never again. This must be controlled."
seemed their failure of analysis
reduced to a question of payment.

This was not the same as a sudden disgorgement.

The owner was much taller in his fear of public spectacle.
Or the function of service, a hierarchy ignored.

The owner of the machine was not traceable.
We stood in line and this was not so bad.

*

That depth is a good thing, a desirable.
And thus the basso, so assuring.

Particularly in a restaurant, where a supply of coffee
or an ambiance, or a flame disrupted.

The way some called "selva oscuro" a metaphor.

Her name on the machine, emergent in metal.

A turn at a certain pronunciation.
I.e. they really don't care, the locals, i.e.

Curious, to have omitted or forgotten streets.

*

But simply the name of a painter named after a town.
So an emergence of a certain blue not otherwise seen.
And yes, therefore, a promontory and no
we would not leave begrudging the scholarship.

This isolation is a biological trick.
You might like to call them vestments
in consideration of a specific climate.

Or a river named for a tone.

Would you call prediction order or chaos?

*

That sleep itself isn't a language.
Thus every seduction carries a new set of dilemmas.

Once they gathered the process seemed easy.
It may have been the tincture of history of simply the noise.

But then any idea of duration can induce labor.

What the machine gave out instead of money.

Her name but not only her name, as argent as eastern.

Where walls conceal their gates.
A carrier, a courier, an outside, transport.

(from *Study for the Ideal City,* 1999)

These are the quotes, they said.

These symbols are accomplishments.

Troops, someone said.

The effect is too general. These
correspondences, just gilded,
tremendous in emptiness.

Repose is the compliment of which value?
Distance? Relation? Volume?

We were there, we saw them.
These are their responses, as if
witnessing or cavalry
attended these factors

(from *Sand,* 2002)

Clear, pine trees and asphalt, dry, a smell was coming and I went east, and up, but the compass confirmed it, wood-peckers also near, a comfort to those who misread. The idea of "It seems as if it were yesterday" really means clarity, a town nearby, wind too similar to cars approaching, upwelling bound to occur, waiting for the truck to come, there they are, a family, any family: their house

(from *Sand,* 2002)

Accordingly, a missile, the way they call any thrown thing a missile. The reference to sleep an accident. I.e. what is the sleeper to the person in the dream?

Withdrawing to a safer post, they quickly noticed an activity. Each fraction of a degree of temperature was felt in dramatic, sometimes convulsive ways.

The vessel, the shadow of the vessel, the shadow alone.

Compulsive is the family that has no heat.

(from *Sand,* 2002)

By waiting or did they say wishing.

Numerous though they were.

The apparent abuse the sisters endured
at the mercy of their dates.

It became still, windless, eerie.

What if what they said had happened?

Gradually one is surrounded by ghosts.

(from *Sand,* 2002)

The sound of the gate at an hour when the gate sounds.

One list covers the subject.

Is the returning of messages a diminutive of Return Fantasy?

The role of the electron is different on paper.

The sound of a warning horn when the *all clear* is sounded.

(from *Sand,* 2002)

His initial reaction was to imagine himself borne down, not under the surface of fluid but into a vacuum that was only what he was before birth.

To them the problem was presenting what they knew.

But why should the temporary be difficult to understand?

The lost nickel.

Deflection i.e. someone else's attempt to steer the universe, or admit to what?

Now the winds come up which are almost the same as earthquakes.

Is it the plain knowledge of an unencumbered self analyst
or the blind residue of an age too attached to something it
calls certain?

(from *Sand*, 2002)

Only the truly gifted will emerge from the stupor.

Shunting the vein often enough.

Coming up for air is not the same as air time.

Your presence is more than an eyeful.
Do they know what it means to be looked at?

Sitting and waiting: their aspiration for us.

There will always be a way to marry the interests of some
with their desire for more.

The calm received in politeness.

(from *Sand*, 2002)

It is raining on the peninsula and dark.

You said you lived there.

When the floods came even the routine was interrupted.

I remember crying, even for the memory of a melody
he told her.

Each promise or statement equals a temptation
and yet holding to a story can often create history.

You said they still were angry.
This was more about alignment.
They are the note-writers we never see.

(from *Sand*, 2002)

It's too early now
in the landscape or town you picture
the very idea of sequence is something you can't compass.

They way they place you on a deck
And all the types of things they call decks.

"My God!" they are likely to have ejaculated or said.
Their gift suddenly sours.
We know that separate worlds remain separate.

(from *Sand*, 2002)

PERMISSIONS

5 selections from *Book of Hours*
Reprinted from *Book of Hours* (Piacenza, Italy: ML & NLF, 1996). Copyright ©1996 by Dennis Phillips. Reprinted by permission of Dennis Phillips.

"Lago Di Como," "Weather," "Movement," "Ziano," and "Study for the Ideal City"
Reprinted from *Study for the Ideal City* (Los Angeles: Seeing Eye Books, 1999). Copyright ©1999 by Dennis Phillips. Reprinted by permission of Dennis Phillips.

9 pieces from *Sand*
Reprinted from *Sand* (Los Angeles: Green Integer, 2002). Copyright ©2002 by Dennis Phillips. Reprinted by permission of Green Integer.

Christopher Reiner [USA]
1961

Born and raised in southern California, Chris-
topher Reiner received his Bachelor's degree from
Sonoma State University, and became involved in
the Drift Group of experimental filmmakers.
Among his films and videos are *The Man Who Ate
a Car* (shown in the 2002 L.A. Freewaves festival),
The Wedding Song (shown at the 2001 Videopoem
Festival in Vancouver, Canada) and *Stage Sleep*.

From 1992 to 1999, he edited the journal *Witz: A
Journal of Contemporary Poetics,* and he currently
edits a chapbook series of poetic prose titled
Margin to Margin.

Reiner's own writing has generally been in the
form of prose-poetry or short fictions that are poetically centered. His books include *A
Coward's Libretto* (1992), *Ogling Anchor* (1998), and *Pain* (2001).

He was formerly the Director of Foundation and Government Relations at Center Theatre
Group in Los Angeles, He now serves as a freelance fundraising consultant to cultural and arts
organizations. He recently composed 14 songs for a musical performed in Los Angeles.

BOOKS OF POETRY

A Coward's Libretto (Texture Press, 1992); *Ogling Anchor* (Penngrove, California: Avec Books,
1998); *Pain* (Penngrove, California, Avec Books, 2001).

A Coward's Libretto

Reflected at three times diminution words ring along wealth and strength, strong stressing deliberation, delight, memorial. And so in cahoots at fault against the antics of preposition. What is not obscure, unsaid, looks for the slightest waver, comb thin voice squeal out of control, "Canyon and Principal. Canyon and Principal." Superb.

⁕

Allure presiding over detail cartel fulsome discord vendetta legislature ventilated cue errorless airless lineament dossier owed to catchphrase *Work Out Your Animal.* In teeth, by rattle, in prime focus of reinvention, "you are not at liberty but may move your hands." In what time ties what small cord approaches. One delightful face to bury transcription. Idiot gods graze this brown bone.

⁕

Me, I note the false modesty the greats, the institution of scribbling, and the secret said *sotto voce,* in words anyone could understand, shimmering cost, searching force of temporary in sacred shine. Note she hears enveloped question trying understanding. Aria, overture, admonition. Highest praise presides over tough undercurrent, piquant bolt of energy itself, query's legendary ripple. All things made equal, and some free, she fucks with the force of mollitude, the dangling feminine, contemptuous even of planets, of nicknames. For the big secret, posing as answer, snuggling, whispering.

⁕

In the age of flowers, molting interior years, year with no *was,* no *back then,* nothing to supply story BACK OFF, CAN"T YOU SEE I'M TIED UP Crone merchant on terrace, only looking old with open suitcase bottomed out. My picture dyed green singing in perfect French a simple expression of my (almost) intentions. "The Good Consolation of Art" and "Friendship in Rooms"—and later "The Consolation of Art for All." God's bolt of medicine. The point of freedom: she strokes me.

⁕

Wanted: sincere, sedate, slightly Merovingian correspondent, acidic, magnanimous. Slip on collar. Vanguard of ultimate zoot. Scissor speech—to discuss my own misfortunes.

Talc smoke insists on Mr. Supercharming. His substitute, statue of the old man, a crane now carries across the square, digesting that last *tranche de célébrité, mouche de renom.*

Why, here's the original, organ and all, standing naked, soulful. I start demanding these things the older I get. It says space, rise, talk back to me.

*

Search for prose arbors, furious scratch above chiaroscuro, with me, against my will, constantly acquiring little by little my own attention, sleeping soundly with more life against any assiduous force, looking for my own "form of purring." At which every bit of energy, all understanding, becomes a song of destination. Part of me even agrees with this abundance of "Lost Life" and "Lost Self." No meaning mirrors the wealth written in potential for figure (female). Significant fiction frying predominant search for one indivisible tone. The tone of ending.

*

A room I was in years ago, before I learned the language, above a wide street semicircle from the huge face of a public building. In the language I spoke to myself then, against the widening arc I saw crowds carry statues just like yours, statues "numerous as stars / before the stars were counted." Conduit dove. Shouting in that big, high voice.

*

The protagonist displays his name's soft indentation. Ribs of affinity, arid marrow. Joke focused on the body. At night, several uncertain fires in the distance, toward the hills. I cover them with my fingers, from the bed, through the doorway, in the center of the window. Sparks orbit the statue still suspended. I transport, curry favor, secret in the most magnificent sense, solemn done soft malevolent jingles.

*

Orange outdoors. All semblance of truth spilt. When she came she blew old mortality into the smallest distance, span between the percolator (percolating) and the wooden table (sill). Spirit fumes, revenge of the bass set in ruins of imperial chambers. Stranded! Affirmation of temperament, weight commiserates. Living on the last rib of land. I (my body). Ocean lace. Ship obscured by flags of the marina.

*

Poke and prod the unbirthable. "I'm just a friend, just an *aficionado.*" A pause between question and cough. The singer's quaver an undertow. A moment laminated by lyric.

*

Solitude guarded triumph, slow self fade to invincibility. Dope wind recidivist year, soft patter of mariachi, sore raised higher and higher into perdition. Cinema solvent lay insurrection aspiring to humane. Pisses me mondo. Not in semblance of *piété,* not in rising air, "that testicular look." In mania of sickness. Corrupt senile balls revert to rough perfection. Not the ambience of memory or love of truth or time's signature. Not the appearance of appearance. Not the clarity of sleep.

*

Do me a favor, just this once, against quality procured by moment. The huge painting against the furnace wall. Poverty of the alcove. Apparition of a window, a cypress. My record of hate, groping the old globe.

*

Smoke pours out of the alley. The tenor launches into a long, piteous howl. The action escalates. With each breath he says, "It can't continue." The pretender is granted brief chorus.

*

What is spoken softly, complement against compliment. Not the tra la la's allotted to us, not my own vulgate, not that old song of glory. What beast can alter its own material? Ask me about the fire. Voice, mentor of place. The word that continues to grow. Art of atonement. Wreckage of transcription. The scream heard from the street

*

A final flicker of starlight rifles through the room. I am disguised as whatever I appear to be. Figure of desire and figure of time. Mask in arena. Ogling anchor again.

(from *Ogling Anchor*, 1998)

Possible Punch Line

Choose two letters of the alphabet. Use them to form the initials of someone you can belittle. Take pleasure in thinking of what you could say to belittle this person. (Remember to dress this person in a stupid-looking outfit.) Pretend this person is your rival—in business, or for another's affections. Pretend this person has power over you. Pretend you are the only one who sees this person for the stupid person this person is. Stupid person feels secure in the knowledge.

Who would believe you? You think, "If I could tell enough people. Go to the papers or the police."

Start to see uneasy resemblances between this person and yourself. General details like death. Then what you do for fun. An attitude toward sin. The ability to have other people think they like you. To remember making the most ridiculous statements without objection. Even saying to yourself [...]. Then to skeletal similarity, logo, trademark, travel, sense, sensation, decision. Your medals.

The figure moves in three dimensions, toward you. Coming through! Oh, and on your favorite street. With your hatred of flashy cars. Smiling. Breaking you up into components of your own code.

(from *Pain*, 2001)

Hard Work

I work all the time and for nothing. I work as hard when I'm asleep as when I'm up. I do this even though some day I know I'll be dead and it won't mean anything. I have thought of killing myself, but how? Pills are too slow, and I'd have to take too many of them. I had the idea to shoot myself. But I didn't own a gun or know how to use one. It sounded like a lot of work. And how was I sure that death itself wasn't some kind of job? I got up early one day and drove all the way to the cemetery and sat on an old tomb. It was going to be a hot day, and the grass stunk with fertilizer. I thought my body was going to explode.

Once, I went temporarily deaf at a symphony concert. Someone behind me opened up a bottle of champagne and the cork hit the back of my head. I thought I had been shot. Then I thought the hall was full of insects buzzing around the flowers in the carpet. My face felt sunburned. A flashlight was shining in my eyes.

I thought the flashlight was the sun swaying. I thought I had fallen into the grass. I climbed off the tomb and walked farther into the cemetery. The smell was vile, someone smoking a cigar, drinking beer.

A name carved on a stone plaque, then unreadable lines like hieroglyphics, like little skeletons; and place on top a basket of fruit. What luxury. Wasn't it the Egyptians who buried people as if they were going to a party? I was so hungry all of a sudden.

(from *Pain*, 2001)

No Doubt About It

When I believed in ghosts it was back when I was very young and my family lived in a small apartment. At night, when we were all in bed, I heard the ghosts through the walls, in the apartments around us. Right before I went to sleep I thought they were talking to me, though I couldn't quite understand what they were saying, and when they paused I couldn't answer. I didn't know what to say.

Late one night, my father took me by the hand and we went upstairs to see the ghosts.

They were all in a room, talking, telling stories, laughing. Some were young, others extremely old. Some were sober. They were all men, all fathers.

This is my son," my father announced; and they surrounded me and smiled. I was never so certain of myself as I was then.

(from *Pain*, 2001)

Getting Into Space

The idea of not knowing where she was in relation to what else was there. Intelligence displaced, and where to gesture—or to whom. Without any reason to do anything, knowing without proper equipment she would be fragile as a bubble. She was already a bubble. And these were embers in a forge. Sparklers in dark trees.

This was the escape route, and in the tub she was pretending weightlessness. Imagining being dead, but being bored. Which you would be up there too after seeing everything once. Or would tolerance drop to the point that it was enough there was the occasional twinkle. Somehow it seemed like cheating to have the earth down there, ice caps gleaming back, cerulean shell, recognizable shapes of this or that continent.

Is that Asia on its side? (Here are photographs of forests.) (Here are mountains, like trails of graves.) (Here are reels of romantic landscapes.) (Here is earth predictable enough for sleep.)

And always the danger of nodding off.

(An island boy, only waiting for someone civilized enough to know how beautiful he is.) (Their name for this place is very different.)

Is like static, which is like air.

Sails passing close, curtains rippling. The house is near a harbor, and a painting of this harbor hangs on the wall. And the light in that painting is so perfect and so beautiful. (Who could have resisted ships back then? Who wouldn't have thought the world was being brought to you?) Is like

thunder, which is echo. Ripple

of landscape, roots, and undergrowth, and a thick ooze of green and blue. Flick. (Fly.) Dray sun. Orange streets. Shiver. (Fever.) Ship. (Wake.) Beveled glass. Imagine the

kettle, whistling, and freshly laundered sheets. And desire to pretend to be taken care of here like someone who will never recover, and never know.

(from *Pain*, 2001)

Can't Argue with the Facts

My father gave me an empty lot. And I knew it was significant, but I didn't know why. I was sixteen years old, and I had no friends. Instead, I read literature and played hard to get. No one could tell me anything.

But you will want some kind of explanation. So you might say, "Obviously, your father was trying to ingratiate himself, trying to make you happy." But that's just your idea. And, more than likely, there are all sorts of things you are not aware of.

Do you believe in aliens from other planets? I do. And they have much longer memories than ours.

Now I, myself, have messed up almost every endeavor I've ever been involved in. Luckily, I have never been in any position to do any harm. I don't make laws, or even shoes. But it's tiring just the same. It's tiring to do anything all day long, every day. Like they say, "the clock ticks like a faucet drips, and nothing is easily corrected." Which means, to me, that it's as much as accident to be happy as to be sad. It's an accident I know what I know or remember what little I can. And the difference between you and me is not that we don't share the same predicament, but only that the facts and the descriptions change from person to person.

Originally, when the aliens came down, they let us ask for specific things we wanted. But they were so depressed by what we asked for that they made us forget it ever happened and they started giving us what they assumed we needed. So it's only partly their fault that they were all wrong.

One day, my father looked out the window and saw an alien holding a baby in outstretched hands.

Starting now, all the mysteries—ancient, public, or personal—will be easily solved. We will know what everything is for. And each life, from birth to death, will have a small, specific purpose.

Yours too.

(from *Pain,* 2001)

Martha Ronk [USA]
1940

Born in Cleveland, Martha Ronk graduated with a B.A. from Wellesley College in 1962, and a PhD. from Yale University, writing her dissertation on *Paradise Lost.* From 1967-1971, she taught at Tufts University, and then at Immaculate Heart College in Los Angeles; she began teaching at Occidental College in 1980, where she became the Irma and Jay Price Professor of English and Comparative Literary Studies.

She has written critical work on Shakespeare, and contemporary figures, but began publishing poetry in the 1980s, with her first book, *Desire in L.A.* appearing from the University of Georgia Press in 1990. Others, such as *Desert Geometries, State of Mind, Emblems, Allegories*, and *Eyetrouble*, appeared throughout the 1990s. She also published a memoir focused on various foods, *Displeasures of the Table* (Green Integer), in 2001. Her most recent book of poetry is *Why/Why Not*, published by the University of California Press in 2003. Forthcoming in 2004 is *In a land-scape of having to repeat* from Omnidawn publishers.

She has been a poetry editor of Littoral Books and the journal *The New Review of Literature.* With Paul Vangelisti, she edited *Place As Purpose: Poetry from the Western States* in 2002. She has had residences at The MacDowell Colony and at the Djerassi Foundation.

BOOKS OF POETRY

Desire in L.A. (Athens: University of Georgia Press, 1990); *Desert Geometries* (with Don Suggs) (Los Angeles: Littoral Books, 1992); *State of Mind* (Los Angeles: Sun & Moon Press, 1995); *Emblems* (Saratoga, California: Instress, 1998); *Allegories* (with Don Suggs) (Castelvetro Piacentino, Italy: ML & NLF, 1998); *Eyetrouble* (Athens: University of Georgia Press, 1998); *Quotidian* (San Francisco: a+bend books, 2000); *Why/Why Not* (Berkeley: University of California Press, 2003)

Spanish moss in America

Spindly white threads hang in the greenhouse,
Spanish moss, no host,
but like all of their kind needing
just air, as the grass needs cutting,
as surely as it rains
the rocks in the stream the road goes by
grow up out of water where a boy
in red hand-me-downs dams up a river,
holds an invisible stick
striped like a flag, small-town
American barber pole, his hair
cut flat against his head,
clambers a bit and finally
sits still holding the day
in his white hands.
Of course you don't have to
go fishing with your father but
he'll be hurt but the boy didn't
want real fish that squirmed and flapped
like his own body swimming,
like a dream he's had
of having to pull slippery weeds
from the water for days
out of murky bottoms until
the stream runs clear,
hating mud more than his father
who stood back there
in the garage waxing the car
listening to ball games until
it all went dream and he didn't
remember having a family of boys
but being a boy drifting
through streams of childhood
and hanging off the edges of cliffs
like pictures he's seen of Spanish moss.

(*Desire in L.A.*, 1990)

Pico Boulevard

From behind the glass they are unmitigatedly still
or passed over. Pico is another.
Driving is to driving as from one end to the other
over bridge and vale. Their eyes unnervingly swerved.
Celan says *over wine and lostness, over*
the running of the both.
I don't find you behind any eyes you open.
After the earthquake it was closed to traffic.
I look at the eyes, the sex, the eyes.
We lap at it fearful of running out,
gulps of red wine. He says
what can the translator mean by *over?*

(*State of Mind,* 1995)

Neutra's Window

Behind the glass barrier by moving her lips
a woman forms exhortations. Her mind is made up.
What shadows of silence under eucalyptus
where the absence of mirrors protects children
and breaks relentless cycles of words.
Fingers over lips in early portraits marks the mastery
of silent reading, a conclusion of mouth begun by all
who suck out conclusion from the ragged spill
of palm and encumbent dust. The child reads her mind.
Silently and with the stealth of figures pilfered from story
one escapes dominion.

(*State of Mind,* 1995)

No Man's Land

Between Eagle Rock and downtown drops away
before the freeway loops
and manzanita signs off reddish
in the pale light before rushhour.
Around the curve, around the bend
where no man's land carves itself
into a city frail as insistent.
Tattooed over his upperleft he can't remember how he got it
How he ended up in Elysian Park
from which the police were shipping him
home by bus in time for Christmas.

(State of Mind, 1995)

The Moon over LA

The moon moreover spills onto
the paving stone once under foot.
Plants it there one in front.
She is no more than any other except her shoulders forever.
Keep riding she says vacant as the face of.
Pull over and give us a kiss.
When it hangs over the interchange
she and she and she. A monument to going nowhere,
a piece of work unmade by man. O moon,
rise up and give us ourselves awash and weary—
we've seen it all and don't mind.

(State of Mind, 1995)

Circle

The hawk circles the air above the olives
back and cut back. The prunings lie
next to the circle of ash to be burned
in the same expedient way.
That it looks like ritual or that the hawk portends
the death of small birds
is a lapse, a weakness in logic
the circle perfects.
Black feathers against the sky come
again in a brush with stillness.
The gnarled branches belong to those
who see them not as solicitation.

(Desert Geometries, 1992)

Edges

Is it regret or the edginess
of red asserts itself in a bush
by the door. Comes to a full stop
in what I would say or the birds.
Not so much the remembered as
at the edges and almost brought to mind
eyelids closing or the thud
of clothes falling to the floor.
Light whitens a vine at the edge
of what's unsaid.

(Desert Geometries, 1992)

Just as well

She said it's just as well, as if
it were an explanation for things.
The mist lay on the ground in a narrow band
and the sky made up for what couldn't be seen.
What she'd meant had the scope of memory
as the girls she'd known sitting in twilight
who couldn't tell her best friend
who walked away whispering to the iron fence.
How much does it take before something
becomes something else
as when he takes out the quince
the roots rocked back and forth.

(*Allegories*, 1998)

The folding screen

Then the screen was folded up and taken to the top of a hill
where the egg marked with blood balanced on a rail.
All the guineas made feathers and made the folding up of wings
and the screen once behind glass in a far off museum
where fingers pointed to the bamboo and the peacock's tail
was folded and put away for a winter when the winds would blow
and every exposed wrist would freeze before you got back
and the trees would clatter in ice and the ground disappear
and remembering the silk would become as distant as eyes
clouded over it was then early summer and the rains came.

(*Eyetrouble*, 1998)

The placement of things

Your feet on the same steps
typing it in allegorical moments.
I'd like to think so. Also one's feet on the driveway.
What I said was I like tying my shoes
and he said children don't do it anymore.
Conceptually dense and enhanced by various means
nevertheless they balance and point.
When what I was thinking had nothing to do with
running into the wall which had suddenly thrown itself
across the room when I noticed the whereabouts of my hands
and the placement of paving stones with moss growing between them.

(*Why/Why Not,* 2003)

Why knowing is
(& Matisse's *Woman with a Hat*)

Why knowing is a quality out of fashion and no one can decide to
but slips into it or ends up with a painting one has never
seen that quality of light before even before having seen it
in between pages of another book and not remembering who knows
or recognizing the questionable quality of light on her face
as she sits for a portrait and isn't allowed to move an inch
you recognize the red silk flower on her hat
and can almost place where you have seen that gray descending
through the light reversing foreground and background
as the directions escape one as the way you have to
live with anyone as she gets up finally from her chair
having written the whole of it in her head as the question
ignored for the hundredth time as a quality of knowing is
oddly resuscitated from a decade prior to this.

(*Why/Why Not,* 2003)

Trying to move out

According to Jean-Luc Godard, the history of cinema is
boys photographing girls. The history of history, he said,
is boys burning girls at the stake.

Trying to move out of what's already established
as what it's called and as it fits into patterns recognizable
by anyone's point of view and trying not simply to shrug.

The way out is clear which is why so many cram at the shore
and stand under shoulder-draped towels
staring at the unending movement of waves

or listening for sounds echoing overhead
from the unearthly to the rhapsodic *there she is*
stepping on to the corner of a wooden stair to release a note

higher and thinner than the one before
or mesmerized before the mirror cutting off all one's hair
which is why Jean Seberg perhaps and the androgynous array

of recent incarnations seem not like clones or boys
but more to the point what she was picked to play the saint
and why they kept the fire burning as the cameras rolled.

(Why/Why Not, 2003)

Avoidance proper is a verb

Avoidance proper is a verb conjugated in another tongue
in routine and repetitive fashion in an Italian hilltown
in which buildings wind their bricks in circular motion
around relic fingerbones anchored in silver filigree.
To travel, not to travel, to have been traveled,

and all to be avoided in the pitiless months of rain
when women stay away from men
who stay away from the shawls and shadows they were born in.
So when she came back at the intervals she came back in
she recognized all the familiar signs,
every building slightly to the left of where it had been before.

(Why/Why Not, 2003)

PERMISSIONS

"Spanish moss in America"
Reprinted from *Desire in L.A.* (Athens: University of Georgia Press, 1990). ©1990 by Martha
Clare Ronk. Reprinted by permission of the University of Georgia Press.

'Pico Boulevard," "Neutra's Window," "No Man's Land," and "The Moon over LA"
Reprinted from *State of Mind* (Los Angeles: Sun & Moon Press, 1995). ©1995 by Martha Ronk.
Reprinted by permission of Sun & Moon Press/Green Integer.

"Circle" and "Edges"
Reprinted from *Desert Geometries* (Los Angeles: Littoral Books, 1992). ©1992 by Martha Ronk.
Reprinted by permission of the author.

"Just as well"
Reprinted from *Allegories* (Castelvetro Piacentino, Italy: ML & NLF, 1998) ©1998 by Martha
Ronk. Reprinted by permission of the author.

"The folding screen"
Reprinted from *Eyetrouble* (Athens: University of Georgia Press, 1998) ©1998 by Martha Ronk.
Reprinted by permission of the University of Georgia Press.

"The placement of things," "Why knowing is," "Trying to move out," and "Avoidance proper is
a verb"
Reprinted from *Why/Why Not* (Berkeley: University of California Press, 2003). ©2003 by the
Regents of California. Reprinted by permission of the University of California Press.

Joe Ross [USA]
1960

DOUGLAS MESSERLI

Born and raised in Scranton, Pennsylvania, Joe Ross attended Temple University in Philadelphia, where he had intended to study to become a doctor. There he met the poet and fiction writer, Toby Olson, who, in turn, introduced him to fellow professor Douglas Messerli. Over the next few months, a close friendship developed between Ross and Messerli, and Ross focused more and more on writing.

His first book, *Guards of the Heart*, consisting of four plays in poetic form was written during this period; and over the next few years Ross continued writing poetry. He graduated from Temple, Magna Cum Laude in Psychology in 1983, and moved soon thereafter with his first wife to the suburbs of Washington, D.C. In Washington, he continued his friendship with Messerli while working as a ticket supervisor at The John F. Kennedy Center for Performing Arts. Ross was extraordinarily active in the cultural scene of Washington, serving as President of the Poetry Committee of The Folger Shakespeare Library Board from 1994-1997 and as the literary editor of the arts bi-monthly *The Washington Review*. He also founded and directed a reading series, In Your Ear, for the District of Columbia Arts Center.

In 1997 he and his second wife, Laura Wilbur, moved to San Diego, where Ross became the Development Coordinator for The City of San Diego Commission for Arts and Culture. In 1999, he left that position to serve as Chief of Policy for The City of San Diego Council District Five, and a year later became the Senior Policy Advisor for District One. He was also active in the San Diego cultural scene, serving as a board member of the San Diego Art Institute and co-founding a reading series in that city.

In 1997 he received a National Endowment for the Arts Fellowship for his poetry. He presently resides in La Jolla.

BOOKS OF POETRY

Guards of the Heart: Four Plays (Los Angeles: Blue Corner Books, 1990); *How to Write; or, I used to be in love with my jailer* (Norman, Oklahoma: Texture Press, 1992); *An American Voyage* (Los Angeles: Sun & Moon Press, 1993); *Push* (Buffalo: Leave Books, 1994); *De-flections* (Elmwood, Connecticut, 1994); *Full Silence* (Los Angeles: Upper Limit Music, 1995); *The Wood Series* (Los Angeles: Seeing Eye Books, 1997); *EQUATIONS=equals* (Los Angeles: Green Integer, 2004)

from *"Guards of the Heart"*

SEMOSA: *[Thinking to herself as she sees the old woman in the distance]*

> The years, bring little pain, yet they add.
> Everything builds, somewhere, and takes a toll—
> not at crossing or borders or bridges, but
> rather, the outside coming in and staying—
> too close to the beat, but by the river, pumping
> echoes to shore washing upon the ears, ringing—
> what the mind reflects through eyes before water—
> at a time yet called and stalled, somewhere
> in the actions yet to take place
> yet remembered, somehow.
> Though, not yet—
> and was already.
> As though time stopped, I look
> there me, after befores.
> And now.
> How? I circle or turn or watch or am
> involved.
> She, there, yes, I remember, not
> but feel or rehearse.
> All too often, again, yes
> there goes I
> through time past, colliding forward
> never moving
> but yet a place, to watch
> and call to companions, to look
> and fill spaces—
> not with bodies or lies or even plans,
> but with the simplest of smiles—
> arching a plain back to what connects
> before we moved in, before we moved
> before we.
> And she knows, not on the edge—
> but where it gathers.

(from *Guards of the Heart: Four Plays,* 1990)

from *An American Voyage*

The world green blue in ambivalent sound.
The heat pressing down against.
The will of current.
Strings of palm.
Adagio of fish.
A light step into swim
recovering artifice from extinction.
Even the breath blue.
A tongue held in coconut bite,
the skin peeled back.
Raw fruit.
Rare exclamation.
A single purpose.
A lame excuse
limping for the night.
Stars suspended in inverted light.
Something is not right.
Something refuses to listen –
Speak or tell.

(from *An American Voyage*, 1993)

from *An American Voyage*

Leaning begins.
A slight sway in iron thought.
The nails painted brittle.
An elegant stretch of hand.
You awake to your own wake.
A memory of miles upon a sandy beach.
The sun so warm upon a naked back.
Each step a print into presence.
A single vision upon an exposed thigh.
The lips red, parted.

Each line, moisture for a searching tongue.
This held in mouth –
savored in wide blue's spread light.
A tension on the tip of taut.
You freeze –
Let go.

*

A single lost walk to the edge of dune.
Each foot.
A step into coconut.
Wild wanderings in the wild of stars.
You make a head-spinning turn and stare
Wide open to a density of tropical hope.
Some where a front approaches.

(from *An American Voyage,* 1993)

White deck sandal and chisel –
A face, from the back, drinking darkness
Each blow is within us –
A spark, a chip to fly.
This easy night, a hammer without repetition.
Its maleness gone.
Bursting upon the ears, each chop.
If ice knew fluid.   Blueness let in.
Hands.
Outlines.
Veins of time.
The callused, colossal, coliseum – no dictionary.
Then stillness.
Emerge[d].

(from *The Wood Series,* 1997)

Symmetry in sticks found.
Intransitive as to be.
Each climb.   A series.
Parallel to harmony contained.
An open.
One runs with another.
Forested upon a wall.

(from *The Wood Series,* 1997)

The bark taken off.
Green wood.   Buffer.
Shaved.   Before sanding.
Back straight.
Perfect shoulders.   Muscles diamond between.
Hand callused.   Fingers, knots.
The chisel in teeth.   Between breasts.
Let free.
In rhythm.
Blows.
Chips flew.   The evidence of process is dance.
This dance.   That dance.
Forearms sinewed to the triceps armed.
Ready for en[counter].
Here.
Peace.

(from *The Wood Series,* 1997)

Wood now to sound settles.
Slight the split opens.
Crack.   [Im]perfect.
Creek.
Musing sap.   To speak.
Not of nature apart.
A part
Of.

You.

(from *The Wood Series*, 1997)

MIDDLE: *excluded*

Plain said and said so. Page down tuesday.
Oil wells and green field splinters, this year.
Old world poetry and the wasted paper leans upon the in us.
Dance rapid and tight, enough to notice and not care.
But to do and get done, already spent and not providing.
Your pension is our poison. Flowers & bombs at thank you.
Ten performances & awards, medals, honor – your substance, abuse.
We are grafted, held, and fought. Precious and few, on the mend –
torn, tattered, and made to mold. This rising retroaction
upon the spin, uneven, clean & shaven
This is dirty and obscene. A sight of laser light.
Pour that man a beer, shake the top down. Yo
mother fucker, new order hope.

[from *EQUATIONS=equals,* 2004]

ADVOCATE: *don't wear black*

My muse these days is a lit spoon. Impossible morning blindness. Cream.
I want to scrape your insides out, add butter, add salt, pull your poles and maybe
paralyze your Polaroids. Expose your snap shot stops of this life.
Dried time. Only dried time dear. Your make-up make believe, mold pressed vision.
The mundane fission of coming between. Coming between yourself, these sheets.
Like going North to get South. Or running to the East to fill up your West. Quest on
my hero. Lance me a dragon. Slay me a wizard.

How far out can you go to get in? Go on, try out. Tire out. The little train that could
had a secret about knowing the right track. They never tell you that.
Screw it. I just want to razor cut this rope wound round your neck, sorry.
Sorry for the facts. Sorry for the fate. Sorry the way the cards got dealt.
So, no real big deal. We are we – used to it. Welcome to us.
Post-hype, post-post generation. Here we are post-out looking to get back in.
The out-post generation – raised on division. Schooled on revision.
A multi-media blitz of fractured mind. Sample and re-recorded.
We'll re-write the inside out.

[from *EQUATIONS=equals*, 2004]

NOSTALGIA: *report*

A line that comes undone. Here honey your gun.
So sweet, so soft, so stiff. You're malleable in form.
I ask for butter but will accept lead. Take head.
Your sex excites my mind. Your cheese runs my dog.
For you a thought must be inside out. And act – a divine
scream. Your center hot and melting rage.
I know thinly concealed – welcome to your world.
Now February, think of snow even if your not.
Try to cover in white, recover the not lost. I slip,
hold tight to this shoot.

There are tears in my body. Tears in you.
Tears in your lake. Tears in the world.

Tears on the take. Tears all over and really not a single
drop. Know what I mean? I feel has fell from the inside.
There stays the shell – take aim and launch. A site-on
Your cross hairs in my mouth. My weapon at your brain.
This kind act so.

[from *EQUATIONS=equals,* 2004]

ADDICTION: bliss

With you all things are possible. Possessed taken and sure.
I cut across the day light and write this. A thank you. A belief
round around the other side. Come with me past mythology.
Beyond the shipwrecks I stick my hand into ashes. Wet earth,
Face fire to cool down. I want to wrap my breath around you.
Your love poem. A flagwave to the ahead. Branded and coming to.
The other half is words. Just words. Silence and full.

[from *EQUATIONS=equals,* 2004]

Is it on Earth? Reached.
My piano monks out to this lived played touch.
The wreck of us here. Religion does equal out.
Interchangeable with each other.
The anguish of being: Is Alone. A wish,
I go through. Human divine.
Help yourself, to our hour here.
Burnt ends crisp, the waiting
Us naïve and analysis, an amazing error.
Worship in the trees, spirit speak –
a place warm and strong leaves
several changes of mind: Food, home.
That's all – we can hope, for a simple peace.

You watch, this listen –
The way the heat builds.
Pick out the left overs. Credible, sure.

[from *EQUATIONS=equals,* 2004]

All equations equal
equal.
Together this
Equation equals equals.
One left
out, out still.
Our us, another.
You equate
You You.

[from *EQUATIONS=equals,* 2004]

Jerome Rothenberg [USA]
1931

Born in New York City in 1931, Jerome Rothenberg graduated from the City College of New York in 1952, and the following year received a Master's Degree in Literature from the University of Michigan. He spent the years 1953-1955 in the United States Army, stationed in Mainz, Germany, and returned for further graduate studies and occasional courses under the GI Bill at Columbia University.

His first published work was a group of translations from the German, which appeared in a 1957 issue of *The Hudson Review.* The following year, Lawrence Ferlinghetti of City Lights asked Rothenberg to translate a collection of postwar German poetry, which was published in 1959 as *New Young German Poets,* where the poetry of younger German authors such as Paul Celan, Günter Grass, Helmut Heissenbüttel, and Ingeborg Bachmann first appeared.

In 1958 Rothenberg founded Hawk's Well Press, which published works by Robert Kelly, Diane Wakoski, Armand Schwerner, Rochelle Owens, and Rothenberg's own first collection, *White Sun Black Sun.* Related to those activities, he edited the magazine *Poems from the Floating World,* which included work by Jackson Mac Low, Robert Bly, Denise Levertov, Paul Blackburn, Gary Snyder, and Robert Duncan. That magazine was superseded in 1965 by *Some/Thing,* co-edited with his college friend, David Antin.

Throughout the 1960s and early 1970s other new books of his appeared, including *The Seven Hells of the Jigoku Zoshi* (1962), *Sightings* (1964), *The Gorky Poems* (1966), *Conversations* (1968), *Poems 1964-1967* and *Poems for the Game of Silence* (1970).

Rothenberg's interest in the relationship between "primitive" and modern poetry led to the development of an anthology of primitive and archaic poetry, *Technicians of the Sacred* (1968).

This work, along with several of the later Rothenberg anthologies, attempted to redefine the range of primitive poetry, presenting not only words of songs, but picture poems, sound poetry, naming poems, dreams and visions and scenarios of ritual events. With the completion of this work, Rothenberg directed his attention to ethnopoetics and began a study of Seneca Indian songs at the Allegheny Reservation in Steamburg, New York, supported, in part, by a grant from the Wenner-Gren Foundation in Anthropological Research. His years with the Senecas also resulted in a book of his own poems, *A Seneca Journal.*

That project involved a collaborative translation between Rothenberg and Seneca songmen and the translation of a series of Navajo horse-blessing songs. In this effort, Rothenberg began to develop an approach he termed as "total translation," meaning that he attempted to account in the English version for every element in the original language, including the so-called "meaningless" vocables, word distortions, and redundancies. The result of this research led to his next large anthology, *Shaking the Pumpkin: Traditional Poetry of the Indian North Americas* (1972).

His interest in American Indian and other tribal/oral poetries led to the development of a magazine, *Alcheringa*, the first journal devoted exclusively to ethnopoetics, edited by Rothenberg and Dennis Tedlock from 1970-1976. After 1976 he continued work of *Alcheringa* in his own magazine, *New Wilderness Letter*. Concurrent to this interest, were his explorations of his own ancestry and the lost world of Jewish Poland in a series of poems which culminated in *A Book of Testimony* (1970), *Esther K. Comes to America* (1973), and *Poland/1931* (1974).

With George Quasha, Rothenberg published *America a Prophecy* in 1974, an anthology that attempted to redefine the past and present of American poetry over an expanse of time and cultures. The same year, he received a Guggenheim Fellowship, and two years later, a grant from the National Endowment for the Arts.

In 1978 he published *A Big Jewish Book: Poems and Other Visions of the Jews from Tribal Times to the Present* (republished in a shorter version, *Exiled in the Word*). Co-edited by Harris Lenowitz and Charles Doria, this volume broke new ground in the fields of poetry and history, providing a unique history/anthology of Jewish consciousness in the form of poetry and oral traditions.

Rothenberg's next major anthology, *Symposium of the Whole: A Range of Discourse Toward an Ethnopoetics*, was co-edited by his wife, Diane Rothenberg, in 1983. This work traces an ongoing course of poetic thinking that has influenced the art of modern times, from Vico, Blake, Thoreau, and Tzara to contemporary poets and thinkers.

During these years, Rothenberg also taught in various universities and colleges throughout the country, finally joining the faculty of the University of California, San Diego in 1988. In the past several years he has published several more volumes of poetry, including *Vienna Blood* (1980), *That Dada Strain* (1983), *New Selected Poems 1970-1985* (1986), *Khurbn & Other Poems* (1989), *Gematria* (1993), *Seedings & Other Poems* (1996), *A Paradise of Poets* (1999), and *A Book of Witness: Spells & Gris-Gris* (2003). He has also continued to translate major international poets and dramatists, including Rolf Hochhuth, Federico García Lorca, Kurt Schwitters, Vítěslav Nezval, and Pablo Picasso. With co-editor, Pierre Joris, Rothenberg has also edited a two volume international anthology, *Poems for the Millennium*. He also edits a series of major poets for the University of California Press. Over the past the years he was four PEN America awards for his translations and the Alfonso el Sabio Award for Translation.

The poems of this volume have been selected primarily from his most recent work. In a later volume in the PIP series (the reissue in four volumes of *From the Other Side of the Century*) will contain selections from his earlier work.

BOOKS OF POETRY

White Sun Black Sun (New York: Hawk's Well Press, 1960); *The Seven Hells of the Jigoku Zoshi* (New York: Trobar Books, 1962); *Sightings I-IX* (New York: Hawk's Well Press, 1964); *The Gorky Poems* (Mexico: El Corno Emplumado, 1966); *Between: Poems 1960-1962* (London: Fulcrum Press, 1967); *Sightings & Red Easy a Color* (with Ian Tyson) (London: Circle Books, 1968); *Poems 1964-1967* (Los Angeles: Black Sparrow Press, 1968); *Poland/1931* (Santa Barbara: Unicorn Press, 1969); *A Book of Testimony* (San Francisco: Tree Books, 1971); *Poems for the Game of Silence* (New York: Dial Press, 1971/reprinted by New York: New Directions, 1975); *Poems for the Society of the Mystic Animals* (with Ian Tyson and Richard Johnny John) (London: Tetrad Press/Spot Press, 1972, 1982); *Esther K. Comes to America* (Santa Barbara: Unicorn Press, 1973); *Seneca Journal: A Poem of Beavers* (Mt. Horeb, Wisconsin: Perishable Press, 1973); *Poland/1931* (complete edition) (New York: New Directions, 1974); *The Cards* (Los Angeles: Black Sparrow Press, 1974); *The Pirke & the Pearl* (San Francisco: Tree Books, 1975); *Seneca Journal: Midwinter* (Box, with objects and collages by Rothenberg and Philip Sultz) (St. Louis: Singing Bone Press, 1975); *A Poem to Celebrate the Spring & Diane Rothenberg's Birthday* (Mt. Horeb, Wisconsin: Perishable Press, 1975); *The Notebooks* (Milwaukee: Membrane Press, 1976); *Seneca Journal: The Serpent* (St. Louis: Singing Bone Press, 1978); *A Seneca Journal* (complete) (New York: New Directions, 1978); *Abulafia's Circles* (Milwaukee: Membrane Press, 1979); *B*R*M*Tz*V*H* (Mt. Horeb, Wisconsin: Pershiable Press, 1979); *Numbers & Letters* (Madison, Wisconsin: Salient Seedling Press, 1980); *Vienna Blood* (New York: New Directions, 1980); *That Dada Strain* (New York: New Directions, 1983); *15 Flower World Variations* (with drawings by Harold Cohen) (Milwaukee: Membrane Press, 1984); *New Selected Poems 1970-1985* (New York: New Directions, 1986); *Khurbn & Other Poems* (New York: New Directions, 1989); *The Lorca Variations* (1-8) (Tenerife, Canary Islands: Zasterle Press, 1990); *Improvisations* (New York:Dieu Don Press, 1992); *The Lorca Variations* (complete) (New York: New Directions, 1993); *Gematria* (Los Angeles: Sun & Moon Press, 1994); *An Oracle for Delfi* (Milwaukee: Membrane/Light & Dust Books, 1995); *Pictures of the Crucifixion* (New York: Granary Books, 1996); *Seedings & Other Poems* (New York: New Directions, 1996); *A Paradise of Poets: New Poems & Translations* (New York: New Directions, 1999); *A Book of Witness: Spells & Gris-Gris* (New York: New Directions, 2003); *A Book of Concealments* (Tucson, Arizona: Chax Press, 2004); *25 Caprichos, after Goya* (Tenerife, Canary Islands: Kadle Books, 2004)

War

he is (they say) a general with tits
down to his knees
he whom they call "the mother"
whose knobs they pinch
stifflegged & lonely
like a cloud adrift
past maps of Italy
bunkers where he swallows
the macho fluids
hates the sexual residue
but thrives from it
in the collapse of centuries
the generals
still up to their tongues in shit
demand it
in their talk   frail jaws
& squeaking old man voices
carry across the room
the war   not real
the death of boys   a caution
he is the bride the others sell
at weddings   at parades
he inches past the other generals
hungry fingers spread apart
under their tongues
beckons the young men to his breasts
& prongs them
electric emissions from his radios
go forth   electric flags
& well-flanged lady admirals
shadow his nuts
the immaculate delivery begun
he sings the memory of his lost tubes
blue uterus
the birth of perfect soldiers
mother warriors
a hissing army slides

under his ponds   its bugles
sound a single "h"
deflowered   dreaming
the general drops from a winged motorcycle
over Asia
rides past a dozen skies
spent veins ejaculating
milk   blue sperm
over his eyelids
the corners of his mouth turned down
in gratitude
his blue teeth colored red
the shreds of boy flesh hang from
shining below his gums
the generals spangle each other's stars
they bow to him
at sundown   in the fishlight
"my flank (he croaks) is tubular
"my hand is at your spine
"the ants climb your medulla
"where the sand burns
"orange
"pink
"the final rodeo's in town
"even the clowns ride bareback
"truth comes slowly
"if it would come at all
the wagging old tongues squirm   the squads
resume encounters
in a hole a wormy mattress
where an old man like a goddess squats
the young boys fondle
his dry tits
he dreams old wars & new ones
hears the sly plunk of mandolines
over the Gulf of Suez

(from *New Selected Poems,* 1986)

The Case for Memory

I was amok & fearless
twice deceived
for which I sought out
satisfactions
in a tree. Too carelessly
I reached for love
& beaten down
I found you
in a froth or frenzy
spent my days around
the pan yards.
I would ask no help from those
whose trust is weak
but I would buy the latest
& the least.
I live for something practical
—the case for memory—
I set one foot into the space
the others have abandoned.
Not your lord or slave
I meet you
in an equal clash of wills
& face you down.
I only touch the ground
on Sundays

(from *A Book of Witness*, 2003)

An Empty Bell

I walk with you into
the little houses.
Rings slip through my hands.
You pierce your tongue
for love.

How bright the fields grow
yellow blue & red
this morning
where the owl's prey drops down.
Look at me.
Be first.
The others will come through
in shallow order.
Someone not a king
is fancier
a thief among a thousand
shattered crosses.
Elsewhere
broken columns
flutist on a hill
old man who lugs a basket
two old men who push
a stone door into place.
A line of walkers
riders
coming up the road.
I blow a whistle.
Then I bang your teapot
like an empty bell.

(from *A Book of Witness*, 2003)

The Last Friend

The day the last friend
dies
we sit alone.
A visitor
from outer space
tries hard
to summon us.

Someone says
EAT DEATH.
I fish around for answers
but the questions
still won't come.
I take the small vial
from your pocket
sniff it & near die.
The police are negligent
at best.
Nor is there room for angels.
The storms drift in from Mexico
where once we roamed.
The way your chest
Moves up & down
when breathing
is a clear response.
I want some reassurance:
that even when I die
the world goes on.

(from *A Book of Witness*, 2003)

I Practice Dying

I tell myself again
I have a headache.   (L. Aragon)
Even while sitting still
I mine it
& it opens wide for me.
Above my head planes fly
with double wings.
My hand clutches a pencil.
I am wet. I plan to break out
from my flooded cell.

I watch the ghost of Louis Aragon
walking in the courtyard
spitting
searching for abominable meaning.
My hands are on her belly
as in life. My eyes
skip over what I cannot see.
I practice dying
as the time draws nigh.
Stones press into my feet
the more I walk
then when the morning starts
the streets are dark
with strangers.
I am riding on a ferris wheel
& see it all.
It little comforts me
to hear their songs
& less to sing them.
I tell myself
I have to get some air.
The songs are songs
the words are useless
but persist.
I cannot drive them
from my mind.
A thousand drownded
that was never born.

(from *A Book of Witness*, 2003)

I-Songs Exist

i-songs exist,   (I. Christensen)
& I have sought them,
playing an empty hand.
i is your mother,
is a good day
& also not.
i equals nothing
in the game of numbers
where it is also ten
& jew.
i is a womb
a belly
something stolen
heart & hand.
i eats
& will be eaten.
i is a habitation.
i is go & good.
i is a power.
i is to God
a question.
i is willing.
i is i-am
but stands confused.
i is a name for ice.
i is an end.

(from *A Book of Witness,* 2003)

A Little Thought

I almost said the bird   (D. Antin)
but meant the word.
Instructions to the police
flew back at me
a great impediment
to public speech.
My doubts were commonplace.
I pounced but did not
bare my claws.
What I would tear off
in a clump
would stay asunder,
a little thought that
filled the world.
Not sanctified
nor wronged
I was their harbinger.
I planned the dreaded evening.
Turmoil on the bridge.
A suit of clothes
minus a body.
I almost said a word
but meant a bird
& ducked it.
I will offer up
no hostages
to fortune.
My right hand
& your left
are linked
in photos   piped
around the globe.
I want my likeness back
because I am not
me without it.

Daft or not
I doze here, waiting
for my flesh
to be interred.
I almost said *absurd*
& meant it.

(from *A Book of Witness,* 2003)

Mark Salerno [USA]
1956

Born in New York City in 1956, Mark Salerno grad-
uated from Columbia University, and received his
M.F.A. at Otis College of Art & Design. Beginning
in the 1990s, he published his poetry in numerous
small journals, including *Exquisite Corpse*, *Fell
Swoop*, *Jejune*, *Ribot*, *Shank Possum*, and *sub-TER-
RAIN*. From 1993 to 1999 he edited the noted liter-
ary and art magazine Arshile, during which time he
also published his first collection of his own work,
Hate (1995). *For Revery* followed in 2000, and over
the next four years he published two further collec-
tions, *Method* (2002) and *So One Could Have*
(2004). He currently lives in the Hollywood section
of Los Angeles.

DOUGLAS MESSERLI

BOOKS OF POETRY

Hate (Los Angeles: 96 Tears Press, 1995); *For Revery* (Davis, California: a+bend press, 2000);
Method (Great Barrington, Massachusetts, 2002); *So One Could Have* (Los Angeles: Red Hen
Press, 2004).

Trading Fours

Barren for broken so might as well
sky up in the not too distant thighs
O grievous angle these pieces seem
where a juncture of two like souls
might color in the planets and airy stars
it's a buddy movie the central character
I want my cowboys to sound like I think
cowboys should sound like in my methods
I loved the repeat the insistent and
anything technical shaping in my clutch
a falling apart heart animadversions
at the boat show in fact a boat load
here a more foreign sounding name
dirty dirty stage direction he sleeps.

(from *Method*, 2002)

Method

Scour the dross say
what seems real alive
you're alone O broken
hearted melody O fly
in the paradoxical ointment
a person is unevenly
loved and yet these
glinting and burnished
surfaces seem always to
tilt and throw back the
light without purpose
I admire that saving up

that scrupulously main-
tained day followed by
a next and a next when where
something else is then said.

(from *Method*, 2002)

Shanghaied

Of the thousand injuries I had borne
I was charging but that light
gave me permission to be powdery
in the dim or messy to review then
a congenial mode of thought for me
was rowdy in my clutch whereas
my enemies for there are present
of smug contempt merely depictive
I'm gonna flush 'em out citizens
definition of the end of company
and merely human care so long I'd
wanted say a simple or a hand holding
whatever and if two people give up
while overhead the planets and
innumerable tiny stars.

(from *Method*, 2002)

The Crown Collapsed

A congenial mode of thought for
me is drumming there is not plot
in painting so that time not draw
the color from how much more if
wrong loose if wavering modern
my heart a hoax of mere obsession

I love I miss blah blah blah
the central character in the film
for an art that would be more
of reverie surface or glowy beveled
the joy was hard to say words and
delusions to be thought of as desire
the way her hands say or the simple
small-town in a world gone wrong.

(from *Method*, 2004)

Essay

Greensward yellow linen anything
flutter of her hands gesturing and
another day beyond what I can take
is this the power of wanting or is
this the flimsy flimflam of memory
everything comes back except the
flint in her the gaudy casting about
for vocabulary noises like light on
the Fox lot years ago conditioned
no doubt by the arrangements is love
mocked to be put to this use still
ever the still image of her standing
there while all around a chaos of
furious sunlight shattered spangles.

(from *So I Could Have*, 2004)

Insert

In my book of accusations and the record
of my experience the sheriff must choose
between he movie and what's happening

O ever-fixed mark O befuddled longing
to conjure up the negative of what I am
the artist begins by speaking to others
as described on page after page of whatever
it was rich idylls the rainment of my heart
the way she held her hands in the picture
the passing moments I'd given my life to
for wasn't I my Lucky Pierre style a dawdle
to amuse this pretty pie this young cutie girlt
here is a dream I have where I sail away
or set aside rewrite and abjure all else.

(from *So I Could Have*, 2004)

Coda

Sky high into the mile high or sky up
she said nice little town you got here
sheriff with eyes on the stranger logic
wanted the big hit the big grab and skip
over the border it's a helluva country
to be modern in cottonwoods and damp cuffs
a building falls down by the sky stays put
pinned to its place with apologies to
those who mourn for chicken in a chicken
restaurant I missed you at lights out
O list of words you seem real to me
wading a little in this warm bath of light
the sheriff remains isolated but sticks
and things fall from the flawless sky.

(from *So I Could Have*, 2004)

Standard Schaefer [USA]
1971

Standard Schaefer was born in Houston, Texas in
1971. His father was an office furniture/equipment
salesman and eventually became a fanchisee for an
office supply manufacturer. His mother was a
teacher, translator, and a secretary for a Chilean
based pipeline manufacturer.

In 1992, after working for the Public Broadcast
Systems, Schaefer moved to Los Angeles to attend
Occidental College. There he encountered the poet
Martha Ronk, and studied poetry and fiction with
Dennis Phillips and Douglas Messerli. He graduat-
ed Magna Cum Laude, with a B.A. in English and
Comparative Literature in 1995. In 1997 he took a
Master of Professional Writing degree from the University of Southern California. In 1998 he
worked temporarily as an editorial assistant for *Filmmaker Magazine,* and throughout the late
1990s and early 2000s he worked for various small businesses from wine importers to dog
grooming. In 2001 he developed his own marketing and ad copy business, Schaefer
Enterprises, concentrating on food distribution and real estate development. More recently,
he joined the staff of *Just Dissent,* an organization that protects civil liberties. He also has
taught at Otis College of Art.

In 1997 he began, with Evan Calbi, an important Los Angeles literary magazine, *Rhizome,*
which lasted for four issues through 2000. Like many other Angeleno publications, it com-
bined a wide range of American poetry with the work of international figures and contained
extensive reviews. With the closure of that magazine, he worked as co-editor, with Paul
Vangelisti, for *Ribot: A Journal of the Arts.* He also edited Vangelisti's selected poems for
Agincourt in 2001. He is currently the non-fiction editor of the Otis College of Art & Design
journal, *The New Review of Literature.*

In 1999 his book of poetry, *Nova,* was selected as a winner of the National Poetry Series
and was published by Sun & Moon Press in 2001. Forthcoming from Agincourt is a new book
of poetry, *Water & Power.* His poems, fiction and essays have appeared in numerous maga-
zines.

BOOKS OF POETRY

Nova (Los Angeles: Sun & Moon Press, 2001); *Water & Power* (New York: Agincourt Press,
2005)

Wave

The storms of concession and the little viruses they keep warm
the way virtue or confession never could
only a crenellation both upbeat and feral
a particle of ragtime, rose of success plucked
the text and totem were in recession, so syllables grew wicks and added value,
but the rusty valve of night might well turn out eternal
if space does not occupy space, only this crazy kindness
like a tendril brushed too quick, when actually it had been blazing
    all that time
and somehow, we held hope in poppies
to outgrow their allegories and fame, maybe forget
but a face keeps appearing, ruffles our shy, ship-like trance,
dark and singular as a petitioner who braves the outside
just to stand beside the sliding glass of time
on these jittery, preoccupied mornings
when one awakens to remember the leader's name.
Dull and exhausted, the old red dragon was maimed,
part by parting part, sez this fresh young paradigm,
zipping and unzipping her rocket.

(1998)

My Headache

Aspiriin in the forebrain,
blooming magnolia
eclipsed by substance
elated in revision
but paralyzed in parenthesis
an aftermath of ellipsis
or moon looming over rent promised
or the destruction of California
long overdue like relatives and residuals
but smart as a stripe, ripe as a neuron

eager to explain simple music
a syllable at a time to elegant ladies
streaked in orange, hedged
between naps
when the dear genius
arrives to clear the shrubs
to the second freeway,
symbol of the one brick is still in place
the old man dreaming of another drink
no pupils no particle of light
print out of nothing
to die causa sui in a line of nights,
preoccupied with the taxis that take him apart
one ant, then an aurora through the thorax
steeple vanished, people forgiven
nucleus of rhythm dropping out, steel blue

(1998)

Oblation

Half-hurled out the window, seemingly by my own hand, my arms were loaded with
wood and I awoke beside the volcano but some vain hope of quelling the awful
buzzing between where I was and where I was not assured me that the state of tran-
sition was clear and distinct in a note or drop of rain, although I'd never been fond
of music, especially when flowing toward the bearer of the big cigar or the large pot
of soup called proof.

That's when I was seized by Principal and beaten until I grew to love the ring or was
it the success of success against the brute fact that I was in need of atonement for the
hackneyed haecceities of ruin and confusion brought on myself by zipping and
unzipping my rocket as if by coming apart by parting part I'd evade the invasion of
adders.

But matter had become a matter no more private than cutting the skull out so I
hocked my head to pure statistics, ducking out of only one lecture on the only snow

recorded to offer my headmeat to intuition and quit my quibbling over distinctions between choice and selection

But what an asp I'd been all that talk about emptiness at the core what slithers off beat when all of history is a colon to nature only a little less than lustful, a little less than final having long since given up on applause, settling instead for ovation.

(from *Nova,* 2001)

Deep Throat, Declined

When like palms the doors of the apothecary pry open—

My hand fumbles past the figs and poultry to pluck a passion fruit
color and shape of the most famous homeopath any white dress ever
    knew though so old it came apart before the eyes

all I remember is the sting of silver nitrate then swallowed up in
    cowboy boots with the hope of turning blue, but it was and
    was not you who passed
out in the grass a full three hours, more a question of address
if just to confirm the position of things, lest we are served another
    hilly-billy king whose
context has gone madly insufficient, not like
liberty or pride, but the ghost of them
breathing their echoes into our ovals,
caught in the throat, and beating more officious than
the continuous questions of how long coming from the south or
how much jade on the trail home
when there is no girl with face of jade, no boy blue beneath
the heavens, blankets, heavens again
marshalling against that western light to greet the widow of the
    apparatus who waits at the end for an end to her wait
spreading like dementia across an otherwise
promising book everyone had found and put back, although once or
    twice hobble back up—intoxicated—to tear it apart.

Followed instead the pithy comet that struck the helmet and swung
    out of bounds,
the moon in tow, so that it could not possibly be a question of
    coming together
or whether pleasure causes pleasure, but who's filling the script

if there be any difference that gives the slip.

(from *Nova*, 2001)

Over

Tapped out in a long hall

what careens out of the emptiness but disapproval or pleas
take the stairwell
it's only the terrible sound of ordinary language
singing through the exit wound
do not transfer into drowsiness
who do you work for that you are not so drowsy or well-versed in
    transferring out
how do you warble
and how may I eat the lily beneath your instructions when you
    have ghost on your breath and lisp a face?

My former employer, is it that participation precedes the value of
    work or does participation precede awareness
when it is all corrupt sky stiffening up beneath creases and pleats,
    creases
and pleats of ink and fusion

And yet there remains first rain, then intuition

they come and get us or is the abstraction all a form of drowsiness

I sleep in my boots and the days pass right over me, except for
      here and there
when I peak out the envelop, complicit
or fumble toward the pulse and perforation in the distance but
      farewell to the teal lows, carbonation at the cliff of a mirage
farewell to sorting us out, to *telos*
and farewell
to the caboose the color and shape of broth
unless the property of visibility could muster the weight to bring
      down at least the visibility of property, if its painstaking
      nonchalance wouldn't be overturned each spring like a
      capsule for an ache that was nothing much.

(from *Nova,* 2001)

from *"Nova Suite"*

Cloud tangible, stars that wobble.

But not raining.

Ashes convoy toward the floor in intervals
the only cargo, a dead moan
or an axon eroding
but the infinite was not a problem of atoms as tiny universes
but of science* as a vibration

entropy as appropriation of work, boards, planks

leaks, widths

a tenth of an asteroid used for an asterisk

always a chink in the infinite regress
effacing the rose or a coat of foam
metallurgic as memory—

where birds are best—

set aside

*"I'd rather be a professor in Basel, than a retired god," says the General over the pings of the pinball machine. The geisha turns and coughs, but the undergraduate persists, "Do you like money? If so, I have no flaws."

(from *Nova*, 2001)

PERMISSIONS

"Wave" and "My Headache"
Reprinted from *Ribot: over* 60 *under* 30 (1998)

"Oblation," "Deep Throat, Declined," "Over" and selection from "Nova Suite"
Reprinted from *Nova* (Los Angeles: Sun & Moon Press, 2001). ©2001 by Standard Schaefer. Reprinted by permission of Sun & Moon Press.

John Thomas [USA]
1930-2002

Born and raised in Baltimore, John Thomas came
to Los Angeles in 1959, arriving in Venice, or what
was then called Venice West, one of the thriving
"Beat" communites. Thomas also lived, for some
years in the early 1960s, in San Francisco and north-
ern California, before returning to Los Angeles in
1965. Among his several books are *john thomas john
thomas* (1972), *El vecchio Strawinsky prova con
corchestra* (1975), *Epopoeia and the Decay of Satire*
(1976), and (with Robert Crosson and Paul
Vangelisti), *Abandoned Latitudes* (1983).

BOOKS OF POETRY

john thomas john thomas (Los Angeles: Red Hill Press, 1972); *Il vecchio Strawinsky prova con
orchestra* (Torino, Italy: Edizioni Geiger, 1975); *Epopoeia and the Decay of Satire* (Los Angeles:
Red Hill Press, 1976); *from Patagonia* in *Abadoned Latitudes* (with Robert Crosson and Paul
Vangelisti) (San Francisco: Invisible City, no. 3, 1983).

Underwater Interlude

fast in the grip
of the starfish
fifty fathoms down
I feel the pulse
deep inside her my lips
on the arch of her foot I
see the day flow away
like a slow fuse and up
up faraway up there
quiver the great blue screens!

(from *Temblor*, 1985)

They're Wrong to Call It the Little Death and To Hell with the Here and Now

> *"I do not believe in the witchcraft*
> *she practices on me...."*
> —Caravaggio

we take our pleasure, it is dark and regal
and strange, she could be Guinivere
risking Hell and her crown an damn their eyes
it's worth it ten times over and I
I hope to die at the last thrust lost
in her smell of sweat and vanilla we pause
I want her again but we pause and
casually she tears off a toenail
drawing blood then slyly tucks it
under my mattress: scary but
so moving: Guinivere
to the life

then she shifts a lazy shoulder and
Tara Tintagel Lyonesee the
whole damned Bronze Age
rolls up against me
her fingers lace into mine
on the wet tuft of her sex I
want her again our two hands become
one great paw I'm into her again
don't know where any longer but
into her Christ! is this Africa?
I smell blood and grass I search
her face as I come the lioness
glows in the antelope's eye

(from *Temblor*, 1985)

As I Write These Words

Things keep happening, you know. As I write
these words, Hannibal is still crossing the Alps;
Billie Holliday still sings "For All We Know"
at the old Five Spot. The dam is broken,
and the great slow muddy flood swells behind me
in ponderous pursuit. The same flower
blooms and blooms again, forever. Endlessly,
I scrub the blood from my shaking hands.
Endlessly, the words pile up, smothering
the poem. Night falls, night falls, night falls,
and I cannot stop this dying.

(from "Lost Inventions of the Night," *Temblor*, 1988)

Nightwindow

> *'The layered dung of ten thousand*
> *years is not to be understood as*
> *different from any rainbow."*
> from the *Kali-Sutra*

even in the dream
he walks the darkness silently
naked on wet grass
among many sleeping forms

ahead
the blackness of the stream
behind
the pale averted face
of a sinking half moon

antique postures
dim and complicated rhythms

he walks in darkness
to the water's edge
where a small boat lies in the reeds
it is marked with the trident sign of Vishnu
it has just arrived
or will soon drift off forever

in the morning
the children will not find him here
where the water flows both ways
and bubbles up through yellow sand
to soak him silver at the brim

(from "Lost Inventions of the Night," *Temblor,* 1988)

The Secret Instructions

This colossal marble head, fragment
of an earlier time thrown down
on its side so long ago:
it rests beside the dark pool,
embedded to the cheek.

Weeds, all youth and wasteful vigor,
mask its prognathous face,
crafty lip, proud life of brow,
the one milky eye unaware
of its blindness. Clearly,

something happened in this place
where I squat, a circus ape in rags.
twigs and tinsel in my hair. Something terrible,
once, in this place. The air is thick with whispered
message, and even apes must breathe.

There are no symbols here (my wishes
count for nothing), simply earth,
real weeds, the pool—real,
one can lap its icy water—
and this blind and monstrous *teste*

which now I, obedient,
strong with the strength of sleep,
heave and tumble over the grassy verge.
The great stone head sinks slowly
into the green depths of the dream.

The last ripples smoothe away and silence,
the last unearned instruction, closes over.

(from "Lost Inventions of the Night," *Temblor*, 1988)

Dead Letter

The journey was pleasant enough, but
I traveled too far, crossed
some invisible, unposted frontier
and here I am, here I have been—
for years? Sorry. I cannot read
their enigmatic calendars.

To be a foreigner here, always.
The language is quite opaque.
Pleasant-sounding at first, but soon
one notices the mocking interrogatories.

Sleep does not refresh me here.
To dream long, portentous conversations
in a language one does not understand—
unsettling. I always wake up sand and anxious.
What did he say? What
did I answer? Too late.

I sit in a café at an oddly-carpentered table,
drinking…something. What they always serve me.
I watch the people come and go, crossing
the square on urgent but mysterious errands.
If I knew how to ask, "Where
are you going, and why?" they would stop and
look at me with their harlequin eyes,
and what their looks would tell me
I do not care to know.

The games the children play
are "wrong" somehow, and menacing.
Are they really games, really
children?

Forgive this poetical touch, but
even the trees sing
different songs here. I can
only guess what they might mean.
They worry me the most, I think,
these trees. I always felt
at least I understood trees.

Soon I shall fold these pages and seal them
in an envelope on which I shall inscribe
some old familiar address. I do this
every day. There is a mailbox across the square,
and it eats my envelopes. I do not know
where they go. Goodbye. The trees
are singing again.

(from "Lost Inventions of the Night," *Temblor*, 1988)

PERMISSIONS

"Underwater Interlude," and "They're Wrong to Call It the Little Death and To Hell with the Here and Now"
Reprinted from *Temblor*, number 1 (1985). ©1985 by *Temblor*. Reprinted by permission of Philomene Long.

"As I Write These Words," "Nightwindow," "The Secret Instructions," and "Dead Letter"
Reprinted from *Temblor*, number 6 (1988). ©1988 by *Temblor*. Reprinted by permission of Philomene Long.

Paul Vangelisti [USA]
1945

Paul Vangelisti was born into an Italian-American family in San Francisco in 1945. His father was an accountant for the San Francisco Board of Education, and his mother worked at the department store I. Magnins, on the very floor and at the same counter where in the movie *Vertigo,* James Stewart takes Kim Novak to outfit her in the manner of Madeline Elster. "When I visited my mother at work, I always expected Kim Novak to walk in," he humorously recalls. Some years later, I was working at a butcher shop, and one day I was asked to take a delivery out to a woman in a waiting car; it was a stunning green Jaguar roadster, and sitting in the driver's seat was Novak."

DOUGLAS MESSERLI

Vangelisti graduated from the University of San Francisco in English and philosophy in 1967, and then, for a year, did post-graduate work at Trinity College at the University of Dublin. In 1968 he moved to Los Angeles to attend the University of Southern California; and in 1972 he completed all but the dissertation for a PhD. at the same institution.

That year he began work as an editor and reporter for *The Hollywood Reporter,* where he served as assignment editor until 1974. He curated an exhibition and performance of southern California poets in 1973, beginning a lifetime commitment to poetry of the area. During this same period he began the literary magazine *Invisible City,* one of the most notable and intellectually challenging journals in the country. The journal published the work of numerous international, national and southern California figures, as well as essays on various philosophical and critical issues.

From 1974 to 1983 he worked as the Cultural Affairs Director for the Los Angeles radio station, KPFK, and there, from 1978-1983, he also produced the "Los Angeles Theater of the Ear," which presented poetry and performances by major international figures, premiering on radio writers such as Samuel Beckett, Harold Pinter, David Hare, Corrado Costa, Amiri Baraka, Kenneth Patchen, Peter Handke and others. In the summers of 1976, 1978 and 1979 he was a lecturer in American literature at the Adam Michiewicz University in Poznan, Poland, experiences which were reflected in his editing (with Milne Holton) of *New Polish Poetry* (University of Pittsburgh Press, 1978).

He began publishing his own poetry in the early 1970s, starting with *Communion* (with an introduction by the noted poet George Oppen), *The Tender Continent, Pearl Harbor, The Extravagant Room,* and other books in Italian. He also begin translating from the Italian, publishing several collections of Italian poet and books by individual Italian poets such as Rocco Scotellaro, Adriano Spatola and Vittorio Sereni. Beginning in the early 1970s, he also was a cofounder and publisher of Red Hill Press which published out of both northern and southern California.

In the early 1980s, he began teaching part-time at several local colleges and universities, including East Los Angeles College, the University of California, San Diego, and Otis College of Art & Design. It was at that last institution where he became a full-time professor, and ultimately (in 1999), the chair of the Graduate Writing program.

Meanwhile, he has continued to publish poetry and translations, *Another You* (1981). *Domain* (1986), *Alephs Again* (1990),*Villa* (1991), *Nemo* (1995), *A Life* (1997), and *Alphabets, 1986-1995* (1996). Throughout these years, he has also organized numerous poetry readings and events, including special conferences on contemporary poetry, while editing new journals such as *Ribot* and *The New Review of Literature*. His selected poems were published as *Embarrassment of Survival* in 2001.

Vangelisti has been one of the major forces in the poetry and drama scene in southern California, and has helped numerous younger figures to find readings and publishers for their work. He has won NEA poetry fellowships and a NEA translators fellowship, and is a respected collagist.

BOOKS OF POETRY

Communion (Fairfax, California: Red Hill Press, 1970); *Air* (Los Angeles and Fairfax: Red Hill Press, 1973); *Cinq* (with John Thomas) (Los Angeles and Fairfax: Red Hill Press, 1974); *The Tender Continent* (Los Angeles: Chatterton's Bookstore, 1974); *Il tenero continente* (in Italian) (Turin: Geiger, 1975); *Pearl Harbor* (San Francisco: Isthmus Press, 1975); *The Extravagent Room* (Los Angeles and Fairfax: Red Hill Press, 1976); *La stanza stravagante* (in Italian) (Turin: Geiger, 1976); *Portfolio* (Los Angeles and Fairfax: Red Hill Press, 1978); *Un Grammo d'Oro* (with Giuliano Della Casa, in Italian) (Rome: Etrusculudens, 1981); *Another You* (Los Angeles and San Francisco: Red Hill Press, 1980); *Ora Blu* (with Giuliano Della Casa, in Italian) (Modena: Tetai del Bernini, 1981); *Abandoned Latitudes* (with Robert Crosson and John Thomas) (Los Angeles and San Francisco: Invisible City/Red Hill Press, 1983); *Il Trisegno 21: the first time ever* (in Italian) (San Polo d'Enza: Tam Tam, 1984); *rime* (with Don Suggs) (Los Angeles and San Francisco: Red Hill Press, 1983); *Los Alephs* (with Giulia Nicolai, in Italian) (Livorno: Bellforte Editore Libraio, 1985); *Domain* (with G. T. James and Joe Goode) (Los Angeles and San Francisco: Invisible City/Red Hill Press, 1986); *Giuliano Della Casa Paul Vangelisti* (in Italian and English) (Mantova: Centro di Cultura, 1987); *Alephs Again* (Los Angeles and San Francisco: Red Hill Press, 1986); *Villa* (Los Angeles: Littoral Books, 1991); *The Simple Life* (in Italian and English) (Modena: Maboratorio d'Arte Grafica Roberto Gatti, 1993); *Nemo* (Los Angeles: Sun & Moon Press, 1995); *Luci e colori d'Italia* (with William Xerra, in Italian, French, Spanish and German) (Mantova: Corraini Editore, 1996); *A Life* (with Don Suggs, in Italian and English) (Piacenza: ML & NFL, 1997); *Alphabets* (Los Angeles: Littoral Books, 1999); *Embarrassment of Survival: Selected Poems* 1970-2000 (New York: Agincourt, 2001); *Agency* (Los Angeles: Seeing Eye Books, 2003).

Event 8: *L'Enfant Terrible*

And the voice continuing without hands or feet arms or legs teeth hair even a nickname. But it's also something deeper and more moving: the fact that even those who fail at both art and life, who play badly in both domains, believe in, suffer for, and truly live only in their restless playacting. Where there is no music as a child but the sound of committing memory to names and dates and holidays. The first time he killed himself was to annoy his mistress. That virtuous creature brusquely refused to sleep with him, saying she was overcome by remorse for her faithful lover of no music as a child but the sound of knives and forks in the throat the sensation around the neck. So the problem, a profoundly human one, is *volupté,* for which there is, alas, no proper English equivalent. No stopping it without a nickname without music only the sound of plates on which the future is served.

(from *Portfolio,* 1978)

Event 11: *Lost Angels*

Magnetic violin and the words desert him. In the air terminal the 60s continue to be replayed. The long hair the knapsacks the guitar picked with three fingers on a pane of glass. Spread before you are the Sunday classifieds bought a day early to get the jump on other brokers. New listings are to be circled in red. Attain the most passive or receptive state of mind. Forget your genius, your talents and those of everyone else. What remains we hazard in a phrase an oblique scorn for the boundaries white of the sheet before us. Known for your long blond hair and unconventional wardrobe—hotpants for lunch at the Bistro, for instance—you have been in the business for 19 years, save a three year hiatus during your showbiz marriage. 'Anybody who doesn't make big money in real estate today has got to be an idiot,' you observe. 'In fact, even the idiots are making money.' Now come to the end of it 30 hands without a gesture 12 ribs without a single sun only the one extravagance a low angle shot of stampeding cattle. 'You fight hard to maintain your feminine identity. Some of the women get so hard and competitive. In real estate it's just a matter of who gets there first, since we all have the same clients.' Said the generals: to camouflage vanish amalgamate with the earth to make a life for ourselves of branches never yellowing.

(from *Portfolio,* 1978)

Another You

"Find a new world; a new world is always
necessary. But I meant a new word."
-Madame O

and which about some of it deserves
e.g. prosody like

turn for this reason
one found finds requires roses to read

who maybe even
who knows or
who when not only when but who

though even the most one finds indefinitely
paying the vague price
sometimes e.g.

But there is however space
two lines to be shortly possible
that [I] [he] approaches

                 .

a willing suspension of apples
bobbing like friars in the grass
what's the score
why always steel blue eyes to love
does it hurt anymore to slice
little women from the disbelief
of yet another pose of roses

                 .

a medium
a sentimentality
of beginning out of time

out of place
forgetting how to seem
in the wide open spaces of
[nostalgia] [willfulness] [surprise]
pick one
you'll never be another you

                    .

in the face of memory
as if something was to spit out
how unskillfully or fully enough
the record followed to the last dot
she says jubilant that she says
that he says that I say that
after all language is after all
is said and all the camels have
squeaked through the eye of your rose

                    .

here I sit brokenhearted
fruitless on a throne of air
to jar your cloudiness
or by banality
your partridge in a pear
my plum in the waiting for you
or is it o you beautiful doll
you great big beautiful
or is it

                    .

turn for any reason not pages
but the sentiment of paper
remember it like a rose
inches from the hopelessly perfect
of one voice you'll wake
and forget to just

picking sighs off the pillowcase
because yes we've got no bananas
we've got none because today

(from *Another You*, 1980)

Alas

false dawn and thunder grown falser
than a glass of spilt milk
a cage a reunion
composed of first lines
where we go from hearing
maybe back to bed or
out the trees through the window
light drip leaves and windshields
gray along the door
ripping muslin bleeding glass
with the bright whisper of a hand

(from *Another You*, 1980)

4.

who can deny a city that gives back nothing back
where the rain always leaves at night
and only leprechauns and gaffers
whistle at the end of a rainbow
who can deny the sincerity of
hot dog stands envisioned as hot dogs
checks emblazoned with skiers and
snow-capped Sierras who can deny

a communion of lovers at eighty
miles per hour shot once through the head
a reply of roses of ten million
sincere words still missing still arriving
to die among strangers once and for all

(from *rime*, 1983)

7.

I sang and sang and nothing else would do
asleep in my wallet a radio belches
a sad song or two and nothing else
I lisp awake the oleander satisfied
I delete the blanket wet my lips
I nibble small hair and suck the din
of what she doesn't say I forget
her name I forgive no one but myself
as many times as necessary
to forget how often I've listened
even for a breath hers mine those burning
songless nights I was afaid she'd stepped
across brushed off that immensity and
left me shamed and gawking in my sleep

(from *rime*, 1983)

15.

today at last big with spring I glance
across the street your missing rosy
lips along my fingers leaves and stems
of this spider plant a livid filigree
of morning the time and again of

rising from the table the door framing
bushy low hills traffic hum the abrupt
and final sense of a boy's ocean forgot
and speechless the oak doesn't stir bits
of green fall from my hand you're here I glance
again my glasses dusty I lower
my eyes turn from the doorway king
of this moment already past fountains
of light at my feet the wall a slight blue

(from *rime*, 1983)

he

If pronouncing terms like bakelite
involves familiarity, less knowledge
more syllables and/or vice versa,
do means like ma, pa, bra tinge the edge
of sincerity? Or the shortening
brought on by wind, a votive and drift,
a stir and an occasional troubling
of the waters? (Not to mention fa,
fourth in the diatonic scale, short
for *famuli*, servants, a little extra
to coo one's head over, like a gift
of mockers learning to fly off the roof.)
Or if in shortening lies a classic rift
between what one saw and what one got sort of?
Wasn't it also the case with anthracite
or honeymoons in June which scholars report
is the busiest reason for opera bouffe
at weddings? Why stop to acknowledge
insincerity, given only mere proof
of the treason admitted in delight
and the will of your trousered clouds quickening?

(from *A Life*, 1997)

resh

Raised its head before it was aroused
and reversed in Attic and rowed ashore.
The prowl of law, at best second rate,
couldn't have had much to do with it, nor
godbeast with the head of a hawk unless
a fonder dream of light. The harmony
dreams not in position, or that it transgress
the bed that fares it, but an ease to abate
flight or dreadfulness to the last moment.
The prow of law (read 'conscience'), weighted
sometimes in love, becomes fit travesty
for eros and other stories, bedtime
or not, when they no longer guarantee
the provinces with a pail of rum. Spent
as it abounds, one writes of ire espoused
to the habit of driving comment
for what one wouldn't recommend, like crime
in the streets, or love as a pun undone for
a host of angels. Is the purer climb,
like music and the father shore, housed
readily in your wilderness? Who can wait?

(from *A Life,* 1997)

FOR PIERRE PICOT

Crow

My crow is not a wicked feast and vainly
monotone as some think or cousin to the fox.
Such the school of ease and ordinary life.
Unless vice versa and bliss occasionally a con-
stant and/or distant cousin.

My crow has a naughty streak mordant as
three or the postman's knee or a hackle so black
and blue not unlike the sheen on the desk after
a day or two of not writing.

My crow is no more ambitious than a care
or reconciliation or dying or being forgotten by
another generation of ambitious artists.

My crow ruggles agony like flannel or silk at
the ailing throat of any odd number, chaste but
not so virgin as seven, spared of all caricature
but himself and the vague charge we need
never to have ridden in on.

My crow isn't so mechanical or idle as more
often ill at ease with that choir distinguishing
love from the simple life, is yours?

(from *Alphabets*, 1999)

FOR DOUGLAS MESSERLI

Jaguar

Deny what you will, says my jaguar, mother¬
hood is more jealous or crazy than you think,
even at times cynical for those who would not
ease that glove. Delicious parts are reason
enough to swallow, modesty or punishment
aside—crass as that my sound—when the pleasure
is cyclopedically as pleasure does, your true
democrat.

Even this jackass rig sounds betimes
monodic, says I, in comparison.

Crab as you might against whatever cyclo-
rama or system of justice, decay, says my jaguar,
is no consolation (modern on its face) like:

shake it, the blind mouse, the crapulent priest,
the domestic engineer, the cybernetic profit, the
margin of guilt (demilitarized or defrayed), one
more model of disease.

　　　　　Lovely, says I, crackup grabs headlines in
the capitol, cyclopean or not.

　　　　　The boys in the air devolve no more hedo-
nist than you or me, monishes my jaguar,
democratizing the craft or more ferociously
juggling the cycle. Poetry or the simple life are
deliberately different, adds my jaguar, cragged
hills and cold war notwithstanding.

(from *Alphabets*, 1999)

Christmas 1999

The answer of course would come out of Nevada.
It didn't begin as a question of good or evil
though something like a demon figured in rumors.
Photos reveal that her rather pretty face was untouched.
Most of the victims, we soon learned, had been young women.
People regard the sheriff as a quiet, nice enough fellow,
more than a little disturbed by events at the monastery.
The odd thing remains the monks' almost stubborn reticence.
As if there's not much to do, nothing really to understand,
just a matter of resolve and letting events take their course.
Most people consider the sheriff right for the job.
Methodical to a fault, he keeps visiting the monastery:
easing out of his car, smiling against the keen winter light
more like a tourist pleased with an unseasonably mild December;
whole the abbot squints, looks down, finds a tired smile
anxious, it seems, to get back to the mercy of his library.
All in all, events contradict the fine desert mornings,
some sense of mystery and dread implicit in the question.
Everyone agrees there are no immediate answers.

It's become a problem of character, of waiting and watching,
as if all hint of direction points to its opposite.
Very little information seems readily available.
Procedure follows procedure, comparisons deny comparison,
walls and hoof prints and books should be made to talk.
For now these questions demand a more sustained position,
something besides a famished moon, stars without twinkle
or the late morning glare peeled back for the purest of reasons.

(from *Embarrassment of Survival,* 2001)

PERMISSIONS

"Event 8: L'Enfant Terrible" and "Event 11: Lost Angels"
Reprinted from *Portfolio* (Los Angeles: Red Hill Press, 1978). ©1978 by Paul Vangelisti.
Reprinted by permission of the author.

"Another You" and "Alas"
Reprinted from *Another You* (Los Angeles: Red Hill Press, 1980). ©1980 by Paul Vangelisti.
Reprinted by permission of the author.

from *rime : 4., 7., 15*
Reprinted from *rime* (Los Angeles: Red Hill Press, 1983). ©1983 by Paul Vangelisti. Reprinted
by permission of the author.

"he" and "resh"
Reprinted from *A Life* (Castelretro, Italy: ML & NLF, 1997). ©1997 by Paul Vangelisti. Reprinted
by permission of the author.

"Crow" and "Jaguar"
Reprinted from *Alphabets* (Los Angeles: Littoral Books, 1999). ©1999 by Paul Vangelisti.
Reprinted by permission of the author.

"Christmas 1999"
Reprinted from *Embarrassment of Survival* (New York: Marsilio/ Agincourt, 2001). ©2001 by
Paul Vangelisti. Reprinted by permission of the author.

Pasquale Verdicchio [b.Italy/USA] 1954

Born in Naples, Italy in 1954, Pasquale Verdicchio was raised in Vancouver and Victoria, British Columbia. He began publishing in his early 30s with *Moving Landscape* in 1985, published by the Canadian press, Guernica. Guernica also published his second major collection, *Nomadic Trajectory* in 1990 and *Approaches to Absence* four years later. His most recent collection, *The House Is Past,* was published by the same press in 2000.

In 1986 Verdicchio became a professor of literature and writing at the University of California, San Diego. He has published several translations of Italian poets, including Antonio Porta, Giorgio Caproni, Pier Paolo Pasolini, and Alda Merini, and edited a small publishing series, Parentheses Writing Series. More recently, he has headed a program in Italy for the university.

BEN ANDERSON

BOOKS OF POETRY

Moving Landscape (Toronto: Guernica, 1985); *Ipsissima verba* (San Diego: Parentheses Writing Series, 1986); *A Critical Geography* (San Diego: Parentheses Writing Series, 1990); *Nomadic Trajectory* (Toronto: Guernica, 1990); *Isthmus* (Los Angeles: Littoral Books, 1991); *The Posthumous Poet: A Suite for Pier Paolo Pasolini* (Los Angeles: Jahbone Press, 1993); *Approaches to Absence* (Toronto: Guernica, 1994); *The House Is Past* (Toronto: Guernica, 2000)

The Cutting Edge

The landscape is moving.

Cut from the landscape
we move toward it
to suture the wound
—hills not remembered
are fluid fragments: water
                    mirror

My eye the cutting edge
upon which the landscape flows;
excised fragment in hand
everything else fallen
until the landscape turns
upon itself, upon me (the space
I once occupied)

then it moves across the desert, fast,
rolling over, smooth across,
just above the surface
of spiny desert plants
digs deep to find the fissure
has always been present—space
into which seeds were not sown

ancient wound of light in crude mirrors
quiet in the abyssal depth

no voices   and a house
not on any street, and secluded
by trees and shrubs; this is the house,
engulfed by the smell of ink,
pen in hand,
I rest in the dark.

Had I known light
reflection might have been easier;
had light known me
refraction might have freed the dialogue

—naked in mirrors, empty mouthed,
everything carefully measured,
hours become more and more difficult.

The landscape
is the cutting edge
upon which everything falls.

(from *Ipsissima Verba,* 1986)

from *"Feuilletons"*

A photograph and your smile.
Mistakes could be redeemed
clutching flowers and maps   a sense brought on
by sunlight   it just occurred to me
stumbling falling for some sign   your thighs in Athens
your breasts in Mediterranean water.
Telling it so far apart
a bland taste of distance habitation or absence
a representative authority in geography

[the upper edge of a space that will never be closed
the indication belongs]

*

A bird calling to itself
calling itself by your name

angelo misterioso

tired of screening out
there is no romanticism
in what can no longer be
touched

Skin and more skin
clothes   extentions become skin

le lettere il ritorno e la congiunzione

finding it hard to keep up; ankles have lost their feathers;
no longer the keeper of languages; impossible now to keep
faith in charts   the sky no longer visible

[a cane brake   occasional expectations lost
what becomes accepted ground   anticipated by its own
passing   the place again]

*

The locality of
ignored towns   every now and then
as when blinded by whitewashed homes

there are no more stories to tell
the heat that emanates is transformed
negation interruption   the meter
is disrupted tension dissipates.

    Speaking calm kept for cover
the signs that go forward and recoil,
line in equilibrium, profiles of animals.

From time to time
and the process of deciphering the angles;
wake up later than ever
to have a look at what calls itself
back; further on the idea of thunder
breaks through, given up by boiling waters
one prelude of investigation toward

*

An illusion of absence provides a key
for the collection of space.
What the landscape incites us to
- the drift defines itself as singular:
never a body doubtless a disguise.

Ignoring the centrism a declaration
and deficiencies; an assumption
of power investment of body and force
informing itself and what must be reclaimed

the desert in bloom   overnight to have a look

(from *Isthmus,* 1991)

Incomplete Sealines

Often a division of guests results
in diverse approaches. You attend lectures,
enter rooms at set times
with your partner or guest of choice

and immediately follow numbers.
Certain confusion pulls events over your eyes.
Do you want to talk.
Do you want to talk.

The field narrows as the evening progresses.
Daughters maybe sons are waiting.
Basic science tells them to set aside
the handled crosses and weary saints,

come toward a more palpable prayer.
There are moments to be cradled like children,
all different one from the other,
which halt the grip of occasion.

(from *Approaches to Absence*, 1994)

Errors

There are ears in the fields.
An easel placed in one corner speaks volumes.
Portable representation a warning.

What was shredded and occupied
by no means sacred to all.
Easy to recognize even through voices.
Use an already existing quote.

Only hours away in retreat.
Talk of the town circles back.
Someone is taking things into their own hands.
A practical consideration: the answer is no.

(from *Approaches to Absence*, 1994)

Impossible Saints

A brief arrangement of miracles,
regulations and decrees outline the sequence of severity,
and trial of testimony, eyewitness
in absence of divine approval;
usually flight or levity is a rule
not of the comic sort.
And best of all offerings predominate,
body parts, eyes, breasts, and such other jealousies
in which we materialize bodies, distanced
from spirit they seem to take a life
of their own. Very little prodding needed,
in a trance the pain ceases.

Saint Agatha's breasts.
Saint Lucy's eyes.
Culture is a matter of subtraction and offering.
the river of blood
no longer runs through veins blessed,
halted by faith in halting
and never doubted the extension of
divine tourniquet to stem the flow:
touch razor sharp icons and sacrifice.
But it was somewhere else that I heard
flying above my head, truly believing,
the chance it might entail,
the opportunity missed,
if only for a brief instant of apparition,
were to actually appear, I would miss it
so as to concentrate on its silence,
on its bright absence above my head,
on the illusion of its invisible pressure.

Each day a name,
and name's sake, and saint's day

every and each name a day;
in calendars the stories tell
themselves by allusion for those who bear
the names handed down by fathers
and mothers; the continuance of small
the role of belonging.

Such reflections are in the end
possibilities of worship and the capacity
of things to darken,
fall as shadows over the sight of believers.
With the humility of an insect,
with the deception of one's self;
a time of seeing beyond blessings and curses
that colour the permanence of childhood.

Racist, sexist, polluter, murderer, destroyer,
warmonger, politician, deceiver, liar,
the single spin in favour of some menacing evil
hard bigot senator shithead.
Self-sacrifice for the good of the people,
martyrdom at a high salary,
advisers and detractors
defenders and offenders;
it's the process
it's the procedure
it's not the issue
it's the delay
it's the way
it's their fault
it's too late to talk.
The patron saint of politicians?

(from *Approaches to Absence*, 1994)

Glassed Over, from "Filmic"

A young couple meets. Obviously the man cannot be trusted. The building is very high and the fall proves acceleration. Varying angels are clever devices. It could be any city on the east coast. But the skyscrapers serve as a hint. The reflection of the sky and surrounding walls in her eyes as she falls.

There are no friends who could witness. There are no souvenirs to speak. Of letters it's the same. A fast track affair. A question of errors along the way.

Sooner or later he will make a mistake. He will surely fall for himself. He will most likely do so on purpose. Set the trap and activate it. No one will believe it. He will tell everyone he set himself up to fall. Or maybe he should just go on as he is. Why should I make it easy, he thinks.

A clever fellow, he assumes another identity. The new self suits him better than the old. He has erased his family and himself. No one will miss him, he is certain. Time passes.

An effigy is something someone else constructs. It can be specific or general. He is not an effigy of himself. An effigy is headed toward destruction. He is headed in the opposite direction.

He wakes up at night in a cold sweat. There are whispers. The same whispers he hears every night. He walks to the mirror and stares back at himself. All right, he thinks, there is no kidding you. He wakes up in the morning not knowing how he got back to bed. Maybe the voices are only a dream. The last thing he remembers is refusing to answer.

He reminds himself
that the story could be written down and that way he would be more certain as to its meaning
or
that the story could be a dream in which case he has nothing to worry about except getting some sleep and he knows a rest will do him good
or
that he is afraid to call her just in case the story is not just a story but is a true and actual event.

He decides to explain it to himself later.

There is another lapse of memory. This time from a bridge. A Pythagorean displacement. A body in a body of water. One body replaces another in his actions. He does not know if these are his actions.

The story takes a turn. It is someone else he remembers. The turn is too sharp and the brakes fail. The new body is trapped in the flaming wreck. This body, and the bridge body, and the body of initial falling are related. His obsession is clear but without reason.

There are no examples that he can think of and none that he can use as a lie. He resigns himself to a bodily accumulation. An average person in an average situation.

(from *Approaches to Absence*, 1994)

PERMISSIONS

"The Cutting Edge"
Reprinted from *Ipsissima Verba* (San Diego: Parentheses Writing Series, 1986). ©1986 by Pasquale Verdicchio. Reprinted by permission of the poet.

from "Feuilletons"
Reprinted from *Isthmus* (Los Angeles: Littoral Books, 1991). ©1991 by Pasquale Verdicchio. Reprinted by permission of the poet.

"Incomplete Sealines," "Errors," "Impossible Saints," and "Glassed Over" from Filmic
Reprinted from *Approaches to Absence* (Toronto: Guernica, 1994). ©Pasquale Verdicchio and Guernic Editions. Reprinted by permission of Guernica Editions.

Diane Ward [USA]
1956

Born in Washington, D.C. in 1956, Diane Ward grew up in the Virginia suburbs of that city. She was one of six children, one of whom died in infancy, and in order to support his family, her father worked as an accountant for the General Accounting Office of the U.S. government during the day, and in numerous other jobs in the evenings. He died when Ward was 12. Finances became difficult for the family, and Ward's two bothers dropped out of school. Her mother worked as a seamstress and for a savings and loan institution.

Ward was determined, however, to become an artist, and enrolled in the Corcoran School of Art, which was then an unaccredited institution. There she began taking art courses and also met Doug Lang and Terence Winch, both of whom taught creative writing. Ward began writing poetry, and with Doug Lang moved into a large house whose other tenants included local poet Bernard Welt. At this time, Lang began a reading series at a local bookstore, Folio, whose guests included John Ashbery, Charles Bernstein and many others. The series influenced several local poets, including Douglas Messerli, Joan Retallack, Lynne Dreyer and Phyllis Rosenzweig, a curator at the Hirschhorn Museum of Art and Sculpture. But Ward notes that she truly realized that she wanted to become poet only when, one day, she heard a local Radio Pacifica broadcast in which Peter Inman described what he felt a poet was. By the age of 18, Ward won a National Endowment for the Arts grant for poetry.

Meanwhile, Lang's Folio readings had expanded to weekly "workshops," in which several Washington, D.C. and Baltimore writers read their work to one another. Poets in those workshops included Ward, Lang, Welt, Rosenzweig, Dreyer, Retallack, Messerli, Tina Darragh, Julie Brown (later a curator at the Museum of Contemporary Art in Los Angeles), Anselm Hollo, Kirby Malone, Chris Mason, Marshall Reese and others.

Although influenced, in part, by writers associated at the time with New York School poetry such as Bernadette Mayer and Clark Coolidge, Ward notes that she was most influenced by Gertrude Stein and conceptual artists of the period. "I realized that poetry could be like drawing, it could be thinking itself, a conceptual activity, and not just an end product."

The loss of the communal house and the closing of the Folio bookshop brought an end to this important D.C. group; and, ultimately, Ward moved with a young artist friend to New York City in 1979. There she worked as a freelance typesetter, and helped with distribution and production for Roof Books, one of the major sources of "Language" poetry, edited by James Sherry. While working on the night shift at a typesetting house near Union Square, she met Chris Hauty, the man she would later marry. Hauty also wanted to be a poet, but writing plays and reviewing scripts, he begin to focus more heavily on film, and began scripting his own films.

Meanwhile, Ward took a job as a production associate at Pantheon books in 1982. In 1987 she moved with Hauty to Los Angeles, where they had two children, George and Jackson. Hauty began working for various film studios, and Ward worked for a while at the University of California Los Angeles, before turning her attention full time to motherhood.

Through all these years she still found time to devote herself to poetry, writing nine books of poetry and editing, with Phyllis Rosenzweig, a journal published in various forms—fliers, postcards, etc. She has also extensively participated in readings throughout the country. With her family, she lives in Santa Monica.

BOOKS OF POETRY

On Duke Ellington's Birthday (Washington, D.C.: self-published); *Trop-i-dom* (Washington, D.C.: Jawbone, 1977); *The Light American* (Washington, D.C.: Jawbone, 1979); *Theory of Emotion* (New York: Segue/O Press, 1979); *Never Without One* (New York: Roof, 1984); Relation (New York; Roof, 1989); *Human Ceiling* (New York: Roof, 1995); *Imaginary Movie* (Elmwood, Connecticut: Potes & Poets Press, 1992); *Exhibition* (Elmwood, Connecticut: Potes & Poets Press, 1995); *Portraits and Maps* [with art by Michael C. McMillen] (Piacenza, Italy: ML&NLF, 2000) [in English and Italian]; *Portrait As If Through My Own Voice* (Studio City, California: Margin to Margin, 2001)

Bust

for Terence Winch

The bust is mine.
A lady in shadows of dark light mistakes, all counting, he's so sad.
The dress the blue granite company of belly covered with lace that hangs
    over the awful.
A chain of pearls to pirate.
Your eyes are part of the roar that can't jump in.
The past, the lovers like sad magnets pull each head into collisions with itself.
Unlike pain which is confronting itself and unlike greatness which is controlling.
Significant that she deals this without nodding.
A cigarette sticks out horizontally its smoke rising vertically.
The wire cutters are crying from my grip and three gunshots (less sleep) in the
    hallway are imagined—a chief concern of half sleep.
A fact is to learn how to think if this his sadness relating back to itself becomes that.
Wanting to speak exclusively pronouns, her mother was wanting exactly the same.
The fever, no longer transferred by hand, is contained in each power lifted foot
    in each mother (who's yours).
The one that could had to give up quietly and without mystery.
Questions are spilt over blackness themselves a black why or less recognizable
    colorless lacking cool or warmth or dimension but paraphrasing sensation
    until we're past physicality which is conquered.
A fraction of this light captured like in a film.
Emotion is located here and you looked and found what you waited for:
    images, specific words, a color so things get powerful with desire.
There's no hint toward the bottom.
A faded photograph is vague as your own memory.
Hearts can't grow to superhuman size or fill up and be heavy like the air
    in this room that looks like smoke or is.
Ancient figures smoking out of time and blowing smoke rings across the
    horizon.
And across towns each with Cultural Affairs like diamonds nearly perfect
    to the eyes that can scan the room and recognize the past, go, without fail,
    exactly to the center of a circle.
Fingers instinctively love the heaviness of a cigarette.
Our physical faults are messages transported along geometrical lines
    intersecting at empty points aided by the sounds of emptiness.
The way I saw you was like perfection because I believed perfection
    was missing.

But it's happened to you for other reasons.
Manners were taken from the table and awkwardly placed in bed.
The dialogue from a film with an ambiguous ending, though a love story.
The more intricate and sophisticated the higher the possibility of error,
    like a machine.
The stakes go up.
A blackness here because this is the shadow of the bust.
Small voices cry out to caress themselves not timid but conservative.
A heart has two sides and can love and feel other things at the same time.
Cigarette lighters grow until they're part of your personality and then you
    lose them or throw them away.
A short word is installed above your heart every night until it's sincere and
    not a surprise.
"I have no home and I must live with somebody else always"
Restaurants on handtrucks, writing on the wall.
Stay on the street and continue the habit to stop becoming as much
    as you desire.
I wanted the art around me to exist as mental pictures.
We're human and have to sit before a lot of beautiful women.
We'll be married women then like clouds where destiny has made a mistake.
We'll be mothers then after the heart explodes and settles into the soft
    part called BUST.
Sequins of thought arrest your face which flows without movement along
    white corridors, doors opening cracks in steady rhythm.
There's no other face that I can speak about.
One thought that comes to mind settles in deep folds of velvet whose touch is
    all illusion and surface.
Whatever country we're in will understand.
We're not afraid of turbulence but of answering without thought.
Ignorance, thought to be wiped out, returns as an emotional state.
My eye which is a circle framed by face, the neck a series of rings changing
    relationship with each other continuously.
The words "I love you" are received by the left ventricle.
You've aimed but can't point there.
Half of the noise is caused by the floor's existence, the other half by mine.
And in my heart of hearts, I lay down, a fixed desire a longing.

(from *Never Without One*, 1984)

Boom

I recognize you as cloisters ranging from mental to material.
This is only, relax, a visual dilemma. One you are a figure
      being filmed on the street arms swinging you walk away.
      I'm my own figure walking toward superimposed on you
      creating flailing.
Discontinuity follows me into the building faithful science
of perspective. The door creaks and what of a place to live.
I'm don'ting   friend   depress   etc.
Etc.'s numerical figures which dance through the brain
as if it were the large intestine. An authentic inequity
this collage comfort/destruction. I'll remind you and your
pen written scratch. Today I pick up stats I forget and don't
keep track. As I fling myself past I'm a spectre on the
              border of glassiness.
Return to that at motion that remains in pastness
a festivity of the body that's without celebration.

So, you play the trumpet in Queens. I'll never hear that.
So we're in a depression, Chile will be the next El Salvador
El Salvador the latest Viet Nam and personally
      Where were we   We agree these useless spurts of
                            a hundred thousand potentially loving
                            cooling biologies
Frequenting stages of minimal sensations with expectations
      I'm a co-exister.
Continue the metamorphosis into my name spoken.
In pursuit of permutation, performance of relying on uplifting
                                 Anticipation.

(from *Never Without One,* 1984)

Corroboree

Almost fallen into a sopor—feet into deep sleep
Dropped here particular spot abnormal timing
Surrounded by history's lips pressed into one
collective eardrum speaking soft consonants lain
down in timbrel vocabulary even Chaucer recalled
as he dreamed of walking alone through the forest
sketching destinations pale next to the lives that stomp
through to you in a paranymphonic self-consciousness
with others such specialties forgotten now aroused
sudden offer to slide, grab at 5 minute dreams
each window in this city of identical flames leaping
out orange clutching those wanting to be on The Lido
those wanting to say I was and I was not there
without you   instead our bodies break simultaneously
become swallowed by talcum powder turned sand.
Jumping large, a noisy celebration.

(from *Never Without One*, 1984)

Say

final authority
appears very slowly

in other words
appears very slowly

a small number of affirmations
each one a scene

come out with it
whispered optical point-of-view

give utterance to yourself
our articulated eyelines match

free of the wreckage
frontal tableau

no narrow plane
of depth / declared-depth

not a single shadow
of verbal play

not even what's
necessary for perspective

(from *Relation*, 1989)

Calm

In the twitch, in constant
camera click, action shot.

We have the right and time,
test of newness, margin of error.

Sky still as wind's
absence, participate in potential.

Where there was freedom,
was still, could only reach this far.

Their eyes, drunk in e—, smoke in the e—s.
Sedate me, narcotic rhythm.

I would say that I do far
from agitation and disturbance.

A sound is my voice,
frustration wanders within.

Ticket to rise above tranquility,
agitation and it dance the calm.

Only with the monstrous mechanization of
the city, its chance serenity.

Narcotic effect is like, so slow,
like vapor, that word on the page.

I'm around. There's peace stuck
on an adrenal brink.

(from *Relation,* 1989)

Hold It

as if in a cave, light

contained, glass globe

if my baby's born large enough

no fear of holding it

our buildings' out-gassing

our lips barely touching

and sore   who could predict

as night came we'd be waiting

galvanized

wires

(from *Human Ceiling*, 1995)

Hold It

laughter emits sobs

if laughs last long

not my fabrication to live in

rough and slumberous has no bed

has parted lips like my child's

unsightly flick behind eyelids' slack

softened palm's repose on other, we

stifled stress, no picture

excluded pitch, no drift

(from *Human Ceiling*, 1995)

Concave, Convex

intersect indicates surface
and face it, hand to heel
stand in profile, fed latches
opening, closing words

the phrase on you is you fed
yourself a foundation
ability to drift within fixation
proverbs and proverbial phrases

the smallest increments circle
throughout the face of it
howl never reaches sonic—for you you
could never fade, dip yourself again

(from *Human Ceiling*, 1995)

Portrait with Continuous Quantity

(time spent over the line
listening

how you think
eat, live

never *having* time yet
uninterrupted within it

not wanting there
not there

mind's eye's flat
design's is deeper

fingernail history
struggle in grime

echo embedded spit
tongue-tied interruption

hunger for place
straight-lined self

its volume represented
as luminous

that I'll never have been
always alone ever again

workers' bodies repose
across mind's fallen building

[a projection of the arms'
encircling]

desire as outrage
largest eyes inked out

in skin
and different now

where face interpenetrates
a skirt skirts

aches to protect the body
when soul clothing fails

(previously unpublished, 1996)

Ece Ayhan [Turkey]
1931-2002

The contemporary Turkish poet, Ece Ayhan, published in the 2nd volume of the *PIP Anthology of World Poetry of the 20th Century*, died in 2002. He served on the PIP Advisory Board from 2000 until his death.

Forugh Farrokhzad [Iran]
1935-1967

Behrooz Gharibpour, Director of the Iranian Artists' Forum, wrote a letter recently in response to the poetry we published by Forugh Farrokhzad in our 2nd volume of the *PIP Anthology.*

> Dear Mr. Messerli:
>
> I recently received a copy of *Anthology of World Poetry of the 20th Century, volume 2,* which contains poems by Forugh Farrokhzad, the great Iranian poet. You have introduced Ms. Farrokhzad to the English reader through beautiful and fluent translations.
>
> Although this is a valuable attempt that is worthy of praise, an un-intentional mistake has unfortunately put this cultural effort in the shadow of ambiguity. Did you and your respectable colleagues know that Forugh Farrokhzad was Iranian? Do you now? And that Iran is not an Arab country"
>
> I hope that you will make arrangements in the event of a second printing to correct this vast mistake and clear this matter. Otherwise you reinforce this widely spread mistake among your readers and also lessen the value of such work with Iranian readers.
>
> Respectfully,
> Behrooz Gharibpour

As editor of the anthologies, I am aware, of course, that Ms. Farrokhzad was Iranian, and that she wrote in Farsi. I sincerely apologize that we referred to her in the biography as "One of the major women poets of the Arab world." She is, to be accurate, one of the most important of Iranian poets. We will certainly correct that statement in any reprintings we publish of volume 2.

Nishiwaki Junzaborō [Japan]
1894-1982

In volume 4 of the *PIP Anthology* we mentioned in the biography that Japanese poet, Nishiwaki Junzaburō died in 1982; however, the heading read that he was born in 1859 and died in 1945, neither date of which was correct. We don't know what typesetting monkeys were at play, but the actual dates are 1894-1982.

Amelia Rosselli [Italy]
1930-1996

In volume 1 of the *PIP Anthology of World Poetry of the 20th Century* we included poetry by Amelia Rosselli, but we were unable to procure a photograph of the poet. Green Integer has just published a collection of her poetry, *War Variations*, translated by Lucia Re and Paul Vangelisti (Los Angeles: Green Integer, 2004). We have reproduced here the photograph that appears on the cover of that title.

INDEX OF VOLUMES 1-5

GREEN INTEGER
Pataphysics and Pedantry

Douglas Messerli, *Publisher*

Essays, Manifestos, Statements, Speeches, Maxims,
Epistles, Diaristic Notes, Narratives, Natural Histories,
Poems, Plays, Performances, Ramblings, Revelations
and all such ephemera as may appear necessary
to bring society into a slight tremolo of confusion
and fright at least.

*

Green Integer Books